The Joy of
MARRIAGE PREPARATION

Tony Marinelli and Pat McDonough

D0910925

Resurrection Press
An Imprint of
CATHOLIC BOOK PUBLISHING CO.
Totowa • New Jersey

Scripture quotations are from the New Revised Standard Version of the Bible, copyright 1989 by the Division of Christian Education of the National Council of the Churches of Christ in the USA. Used by permission. All rights reserved.

Chapter 11 "The Wedding Liturgy" was written by Rev. Ron Hayde, Director, Office of Worship, Rockville Centre, NY.

First published in September, 2001 by Resurrection Press, Catholic Book Publishing Company.

ISBN 1-878718-64-9

Library of Congress Catalog Number: 01-132739

Cover design and photo by John Murello

Printed in the United States of America

1 2 3 4 5 6 7 8 9

Dedication

To all the faithful in the Diocese of Rockville Centre and especially to Fred.

Contents

Foreword

THE preparation of couples for the sacrament of marriage is both a unique concern and challenge as well as the pastoral responsibility of priests, deacons, and pastoral ministers. The covenant of marriage, that indissoluble union of a man and woman in the sacrament of marriage is a clear sign of the love of Christ for the Church.

Couples approaching the sacrament of marriage come from a variety of religious experiences ranging from a full and committed practice of their faith, to a marginalized participation in the life of the Church. Those who prepare couples for marriage are not only confronted with this dilemma, but with the unique opportunity for evangelization and catechesis that the occasion of their marriage will provide.

The Joy of Marriage Preparation provides not only a wealth of information, but keen practical and pastoral insight into aspects of marriage preparation. Pat and Tony have been married for eighteen years, and they draw upon not only their education and pastoral experience, but also on their own experience of faithfully living the sacrament of marriage. Beginning with observations on those who are now approaching the sacrament of marriage and concluding with the wedding liturgy, *The Joy of*

Marriage Preparation covers a wide range of topics, each of which seeks to develop an understanding of Christian marriage and married life.

It is my hope that this book will benefit those who prepare couples for marriage, but also those couples who approach this sacrament. May God's love, which gathers us together, continue to grow in the hearts and lives of all those preparing for marriage.

✠ John R. McGann
Bishop Emeritus
Diocese of Rockville, Centre, New York

Introduction

IN his 1981 apostolic letter, "On the Family," Pope John Paul II urged the Church to promote better and more intensive programs of marriage preparation in order to help young couples establish successful marriages. In 1989, the National Conference of Catholic Bishops published *Faithful to Each Other Forever: A Catholic Handbook of Pastoral Help for Marriage Preparation,* a well thought out and carefully researched guide to marriage preparation. The United States Bishops Committee for Pastoral Research and Practices have since published several documents to assist those involved in marriage preparation, among which are *Making Marriage Work, Planning Your Wedding Ceremony, Our Future Together,* and *Growing Together in Spirit.*

The Holy Father and the American Catholic bishops aren't the only ones interested in effectively preparing young couples for marriage. In 1995, the Council on Families in America urged all churches to establish and strengthen premarital counseling. To stem the increase in divorce and abuse, the states of New Mexico, North Dakota, and Connecticut have drafted policies requiring pre-marital education or counseling before the issuance of a marriage license. Missouri, Michigan, and Maryland require a waiting period until the couple can prove that they have participated in some form of pre-marital education or counseling. Arizona offers reduced license fees for applicants who have received some form of marriage preparation.

Preparing couples for marriage is an important endeavor in which organizations, both sacred and secular, are invested. We're all in agreement that effective marriage preparation is critical to the future of families, churches, and the world. But who should provide the support, the information, and the guidance that young couples are seeking today? State and federal legislation may one day designate funding to put effective marriage preparation programs in place throughout the United States, but in the meantime, the Catholic Church will continue to offer marriage preparation to each and every couple who chooses to walk down its aisle. Through trial and error, and the guidance of the Holy Spirit, the Church has progressed to a point where its efforts have had a measurable effect on marriage.

The Center for Marriage and Family at Creighton University conducted a six year study on marriage preparation in the Catholic Church, the results of which are redefining marriage preparation both inside and outside the Catholic Church. Among the study's many findings was this: engaged couples report that marriage preparation is regarded as most valuable when it's administered by a pastoral team composed of clergy, lay couples, and parish staff. A pastoral team such as this provides young adults and their families with a microcosm of the Church. A variety of vocations, each with a unique gift to offer, converge to serve the Church's essential mission to evangelize. Even when the ideal ministerial situation is not possible and clergy or lay couples have no choice but to meet young couples without the support of a pastoral team, we've found marriage preparation to still be an exciting and richly rewarding endeavor for everyone involved.

We've been involved in religious education for the past twenty years. We've taught in Catholic high schools, seminaries, and universities. We've been directors of parish religious education programs, adult formation programs and retreat programs for adolescents. We've worked alone, but more often we've had the wonderful experience of working with teams of talented people. All our experiences have been helpful in enhancing our ministry to engaged couples. Perhaps the most helpful has been Pat's experience as a psychologist. Her understanding of family dynamics and the family life cycle, her work in the areas of addiction and codependency, and her familiarity with educational tools designed for marriage preparation has certainly fine tuned our ministry. Throughout this book, we share with you our professional experiences of ministry as well as our personal investment in marriage and family life, both of which we hope nurture your ministry to engaged couples.

This book addresses many of the issues that research indicates are most important for young couples to consider before entering into marriage; family origin issues, communication styles, sexuality, family planning, faith, cohabitation, and careers, and the importance of prioritizing each of the many things which demand the attention of newly married couples.

As you know, the decision to marry is one of the most significant and personal choices that people make. Once made, the process of preparing for that marriage is life-altering in itself. You have an important role to play in that process. Your ministry involves meeting young couples and providing them with the time and place to discuss critical and often ignored issues that will surface at some point in their marriage, if not before. Through marriage preparation, young couples are given the opportunity to meet a miraculous mix of faith-filled people who share their experience of vocation, of love and marriage, of coupleness and solitude, of parenthood, of prayer and service. Young adults learn a lot about the people involved in marriage preparation. They learn a lot about the Church, about themselves, about the sacraments, scripture, and hopefully, about what goes into forming a healthy, holy relationship. What better gift to give the bride and groom.

Chapter One

Generation X Gets Married

NOVELIST Douglas Coupland coined the term Generation X when he referred to twenty-something and thirty-something young Americans who have neither a traditional history nor a predictable future. Theirs was a childhood so unlike any other in the history of our society that their future cannot be accurately predicted, and therefore, can only be represented by X. As we know, the unknown can provide an interesting and exciting dimension to life. We believe that many members of Generation X will surprise us with outstanding contributions to science, to the humanities and to the Church, but sociologists tend to be a little more pessimistic. Their data suggests that these young adults are a generation lost to traditional values, to long accepted definitions of faith, commitment and love. They are, for the most part, lost to the Church and perhaps, lost to themselves.

The data tells us that they are the children of a 50 percent divorce rate who grew up in homes where the only parent or both parents worked often and were simply not around. AIDS, condoms, safe sex and date rape were part of their vocabulary before they left junior high. Latest studies indicate that members of Generation X witnessed the act of intercourse on TV or in the movies more than a hundred times throughout adolescence. Perhaps there's a connection to be made when research also indicates that, despite the information available through sex education classes, these young women have had more unplanned pregnancies and subsequent abortions than any other group in the nation. Only 65 percent of females from Generation X are married when they give birth to their first child. All evidence points to the likelihood that this generation will face a higher divorce rate, a higher rate of incarceration, depression, poverty, drug abuse, physical abuse, and suicide than any other generation of Americans.

As the unique challenges associated with Generation X quickly gained the attention of the American media, so too, they became a growing concern for the Church. The late Cardinal Bernardin's statement, *Called to Be Catholic: Church in a Time of Peril,* acknowledged Catholic youth to be a generation who are "disenfranchised, confused about their beliefs and increasingly adrift." The document continues, "On every side, there are reports that many Catholics are reaching adulthood with barely a rudimentary knowledge of their faith, with an attenuated sense of sacrament, and with a highly individualistic view of the Church".

David Leege, professor in the Program for Research on Religion, Church, and Society at the University of

Notre Dame and co-author of *Rediscovering the Religious Factor in American Politics,* finds young Catholics to be less likely than any other religious group to be influenced politically or morally by Church leadership. They are, for the most part, unreceptive to Church teaching on important social and ethical issues and claim that the Church holds little credibility with them. These findings appear to be particularly evident among young Catholic women. This is one of the many reasons why your call to the ministry of marriage preparation is so important to the life of the Church. You have been given the opportunity to bridge two generations to one life in Christ.

A recent study conducted by The University of Chicago claimed that only 13.2 percent of Catholics under the age of 25 attend Mass regularly, and there is a very real possibility that some of these young Catholics will leave the Church at some time in their adult life. Take heart in the words of the American bishops, who in their document, *Sons and Daughters of the Light: A Pastoral Plan for Ministry with Young Adults,* tell us that "young adults will participate in the Church when they perceive that the invitation is authentic and their participation is constructive."

Our experience is consistent with that of the bishops. When we enter into an open and honest relationship with young couples, they sense that our desire to be part of their lives and for them to be a part of the Church is sincere. Young adults mistakenly believe that we might judge them harshly if they are not practicing Catholics. But we believe that every human being is hard wired for a relationship with God. Each and every one of us has a spiritual dimension to our lives, even if we don't have the language necessary to articulate that spirituality. But that language can be learned through exposure, just as any language can be picked up when we are immersed in it.

Often in casual conversation with the engaged couples we explore the many ways in which they have tried to develop a spiritual dimension to their lives. We've learned a lot from these conversations. Some of the couples have a deep interest in the practice of meditation or non-violence. They are more familiar with the writings of the Dalai Lama than the writings of Matthew, Mark, Luke and John. Maybe the Dalai Lama, author of the best selling *The Art of Happiness,* has better PR than the evangelists because so few young adults realize that the practice of prayer and non-violence are integral to the life of Jesus and the Gospel.

Today, celebrities such as Richard Gere talk passionately about Buddhism on nightly talk shows and in magazines geared toward young adults. Richard Gere has their ear. The Catholic priest at the pulpit may not.

The rich and famous who speak emphatically about their religious beliefs and its benefits probably inspire many young people to pursue that path. John Travolta is just one of the Hollywood stars who speaks confidently about his commitment to Scientology. There are few stars, however, who speak out fervently in favor of the gospel message.

We've learned that many young couples have dabbled in New Age spirituality, mysticism, mediums and the study of angels. Some have developed a deep commitment to service, particularly to the poor and those suffering from AIDS. Their commitment is manifested through their work with organizations such as Habitat for Humanity or the Peace Corps. One couple that we met were devoted to the teachings of Depak Chopra, the popular author of many books including *The Seven Spiritual Laws of Success*. Other couples are more familiar with The *Prayer of Jabez*, the best selling book by evangelist Bruce Wilkinson. One couple talked about their background in Celtic spirituality. We helped them identify the links between their experiences and Celtic Christianity.

What is clear to us is that we are all pilgrims journeying toward God. This is one of the reasons that we find such joy in the ministry of marriage preparation. The priests, deacons, religious, and lay couples involved in marriage preparation and education are in the fortunate position of learning about the spiritual pilgrimages of young people today while at the same time welcoming them into the Church, some for the first time, and some for the first time in years. We are helping to build a bridge between young adults and the Good News of Jesus Christ. It's an exciting endeavor and important, as well. These young couples are the future of our Church.

Chapter Two

A More Perfect Union

G OD formed a perfect union in Paradise. Male and female He created them to cling to one another and become one flesh. Maybe it was easier in Eden. They didn't have in-laws and two careers. They didn't have to worry about money or mortgages. They didn't know what stress was and infidelity wasn't even a possibility. Compared to couples getting married today, Adam and Eve had it easy. After all, they were made for one another.

Finding the perfect mate today is a little more complicated than it was in Eden. It's even more complicated than it was ten or twenty years ago. The couples getting married today are older, better educated, and more financially secure than the couples of yesteryear. And yet, these same couples are less likely to have received a Catholic education or participated regularly in a parish religious education program throughout childhood and adolescence. We can't take for granted that they understand the meaning of the word sacrament or vocation. They may not be familiar with the gospels or the feast days of the Church.

Not too long ago, we asked a group of engaged couples if anyone could tell us why marriage preparation was sometimes referred to as Pre-Cana. Not one couple knew. Not one bride or groom-to-be had ever heard the story of the Wedding Feast at Cana. That's the bad news. The good news is that they're still coming to the Church to get married, maybe not for all the reasons we'd like them to be coming, but, they're here, and that in itself is a gift.

In the recent document "Preparation for the Sacrament of Marriage," the Pontifical Council for the Family encouraged "the pastoral care of the family to direct its best efforts toward qualifying marriage preparation, making use of pedagogical and psychological aids that have a sound orientation." The NCCB recommends that "marriage preparation instruments be used to help the engaged couple look at their relationship, learn about each other, and grow in their skills of relating, decision making and problem solving, as well as deepen their understanding of marriage, especially a sacramental marriage".

Both the Pontifical Council and the NCCB encourage the use of pre-marital inventories when beginning the process of marriage preparation with young couples. FOCCUS, PREP, PMIP, and PREPARE are among the most popular instruments used in the United States. Our choice is FOCCUS, a Catholic pre-marital instrument developed in 1985 by three marriage and family counselors, including Sister Barbara Markey,

Ph.D., Director of the Family Life Office in Omaha, Nebraska. FOCCUS is a 156-item instrument designed to help couples determine readiness for marriage by surfacing areas of strength and areas of growth that are unique to their relationship and indicative of their capacity to form a healthy and sacramental marriage.

FOCCUS (Facilitating Open Couple Communication, Understanding and Study), asks a couple to respond to questions about their family of origin, support for the relationship from friends and family, role expectations in marriage, issues related to self-esteem, sexuality, interpersonal skills such as communication and conflict resolution, shared values, shared leisure activities, attitudes toward money, children, career, church, and spirituality. FOCCUS also touches on more sensitive topics such as addiction and abuse, both of which we know can have a devastating effect on a couple if not addressed adequately before marriage. Having worked closely with the Marriage Tribunal in our diocese, we can tell you that the Tribunal officials agree that FOCCUS addresses the issues that later present themselves in the annulment process. In fact, research on FOCCUS shows that without FOCCUS as part of the marriage preparation process, three to five percent of couples choose to postpone or call off their wedding. When FOCCUS is included in the process, seventeen percent of engaged couples choose to change their plans. The

Tribunal judges suspect that these couples may be the very ones who would later be applying for annulments.

A pre-marital inventory can be used as an introduction to the marriage preparation process, inviting each couple into a program that is uniquely tailored to address their particular needs in preparing to celebrate the Sacrament of Marriage. The young couple is more likely to be engaged in a process that is highly individualized and addresses the specific areas of concern that they bring to marriage. They're more likely to take an active interest in marriage preparation, invest more of themselves in the process, and gain more insight into their relationship to each other, God, and the Church as a result of their personal investment in the program, therefore increasing the long term effectiveness of marriage preparation. It's important to remember that FOCCUS is not used to determine whether a couple will be allowed to marry in the Church, but to help each couple identify their strengths and the areas where growth is needed.

FOCCUS can be administered by a priest, deacon, or sponsor couple (a married couple who will accompany the engaged couple through the marriage preparation process). It can be administered in a group or individually, however, the feedback is always given privately. Members of the marriage preparation team will be trained to take on one of two roles when providing feedback for FOCCUS. The first role is that of facilitator. The facilitator helps facilitate communication between the couple, directing their attention to sharing thoughts and feelings with each other and working toward solutions to some of the issues raised, if possible. At other times, the person or couple providing feedback from FOCCUS will be called upon to teach. Teaching might take the form of modeling a communication strategy or explaining the Church teaching on family planning or the meaning of a sacrament.

The first few times that we administered FOCCUS to engaged couples, everything went smoothly. The couples differed in communication styles and problem solving techniques. The bride and groom sometimes disagreed about shared time and dual careers, religious practice or who would manage their money. At times we facilitated conversation between the couple. At other times we took on the role of a teaching couple.

Nick and Chelsea could not resolve their difficulties concerning household responsibilities. We stepped in. "Can we share with you how we handled this same conflict in our relationship?" We talked about the ways in which we found it most helpful to divide up the household chores.

We certainly don't have the answer to everyone's problems. We don't even have the answers to our problems. But some issues seem to be universal and present themselves in almost every marriage. For those situations, offering some practical suggestions might help the couple to resolve their problems by gaining insight into how other couples have tried to resolve the same problems. The engaged couple will learn to brainstorm the possible ways in which a particular problem can be addressed.

Mike and Megan

When we met with Mike and Megan, things were different. FOCCUS was able to surface a concern that Megan had about Mike's drinking, a concern that Mike didn't want to talk about.

Megan's response to one of the FOCCUS questions indicated that the use of alcohol had caused problems between them. She had tried to raise this issue with Mike in the past, but he quickly moved away from the conversation, denying that alcohol could be the source of the problems between them. When we met with Mike and Megan to provide feedback from FOCCUS, Mike became irritated when the topic of his drinking was raised. He said Megan was making too much of his good times. He thought that the problems in their relationship stemmed more from Megan's moodiness than his desire to have fun.

One of the hallmarks of addiction is denial. Mike had grown up with an alcoholic father but was certain that he was not like his father. Mike was sure that he had his drinking under control, even when Megan pointed to violent arguments that had taken place between them when Mike was drinking. During our feedback session with this couple, we encouraged Megan to express her feelings about Mike's use of alcohol. Mike listened. He was not able to dismiss Megan as easily as he had in the past. Our session together provided the couple with the opportunity to discuss sensitive issues in a safe environment. Megan felt supported by our presence and we became acutely aware that this couple had special needs that might not have surfaced in a group session with other engaged couples.

We provided Mike and Megan with some literature about addiction. We also asked the pastor to suggest the name of a therapist who specialized in addictive/co-dependent issues.

As it turns out, Mike and Megan never contacted the therapist. They broke off their engagement six weeks later. They were unable to resolve this issue as well as others pertaining to their leisure time and shared values.

FOCCUS is designed to surface issues specific to each couple's unique history and present relationship. We've found FOCCUS to be extremely helpful in preparing couples, not just for marriage, but for *their* marriage. So why isn't everyone using FOCCUS?

Let's face it, change is never easy. Change tends to surface anxiety about who we are and the value of what we do. We've encountered couples who have been involved in marriage preparation for 25 years and are still using the same hand-outs. They believe that their program is effective. Unfortunately, the research doesn't back their belief. That's not to say that marriage preparation through the years hasn't provided a wonderful form of ministry to the engaged couples who participated in parish and diocesan programs. It opened the door to evangelization and education, as well as an experience of Christian community. However, if ministry is to be effective, it has to change to meet the needs of a changing population.

We've worked with both priests and married couples who were uncomfortable with the direct approach of FOCCUS. We've met members of marriage prep teams that have felt that the intimacy of the questions was unnecessary. "This is ministry, not science," one priest said to us. Asking people to change the way that they have ministered to engaged couples for years can be threatening. But watch where those feelings of insecurity are projected. "FOCCUS will offend the engaged couples," one married couple said. That's always a possibility, although it has not been our experience. More often than not we've found that some members of marriage preparation teams have not dealt with their own issues of addiction or sexuality and are therefore uncomfortable with some of the issues raised by FOCCUS. It's important to identify where the discomfort lies so that the root of the anxiety can be examined.

We're fortunate to live in a time when we have tools that can assist engaged couples in raising difficult subjects and considering them seriously with the guidance of dedicated ministers before marriage rather than struggling to understand these difficulties on their own after marriage.

Making Referrals

One question that is often raised by people administering and providing feedback for FOCCUS is this: What do we do if a serious problem surfaces? The members of a marriage preparation team are often not mental health professionals, nor are they expected to be. We suggest that the pastor or the members of the marriage prep team provide referrals for the couples who are struggling with a history of sexual abuse or another serious situation that is beyond the realm of a marriage prep program. The task of the team is not to resolve every couple's problems, but to help the couple acknowledge or anticipate difficulties that could compromise the future of their marriage. Most parishes already have a referral list or have the number of Catholic Charities counseling services or another trusted local mental health facility available.

Anna and Luke

Several years ago, we administered FOCCUS to a couple whose responses raised some concerns about their sexual relationship. Anna's answer sheet indicated that she was raised in a family that did not have positive attitudes about sex and that a past sexual experience could affect her relationship with her spouse in a negative way. During our feedback session, we asked Anna about those responses. She said that she had been repeatedly raped by her mother's boyfriend when she was a child. Her mother told her not to tell anyone. No treatment was ever sought.

We felt fortunate that FOCCUS was able to surface this issue before Anna and Luke married. We encouraged them to talk more about her history and their sexual relationship. We contacted Anna later in the week with the names of several therapists who were experienced in treating problems of this nature. Anna entered into therapy the following week. Luke supported her through the process and together they gained insight into the impact that Anna's history could have on their marriage.

It's up to the engaged couple to follow through with the referral and with the priest or deacon who will be witnessing their wedding. This is one reason why FOCCUS should be given immediately after the couple's first visit to the rectory. Counseling takes time and the more time the couple has before the wedding, the more likely that they will be able to attend to the issues raised in counseling and the less likely they are to be distracted by the many details of planning a wedding.

Of course, more often than not, the issues surfaced by FOCCUS are not severe enough to warrant the assistance of professionals. In most cases, the bride and groom-to-be will find that they need to strengthen their communication skills or discuss issues of faith or parenting in more depth before getting married. The couple who are providing the feedback for FOCCUS can be extremely helpful in these situations. They can model communication skills and share the ways in which they resolved some of the difficulties that arose in their own marriage. The FOCCUS couple can switch between being a facilitating couple and a teaching couple, both of which are explained in detail in the FOCCUS manual.

FOCCUS, like many other inventories, is relatively inexpensive, user-friendly, and can be scored by hand or by computer. FOCCUS is available in Spanish, Braille, and in audiocassettes. There are also supplements available for interfaith couples, cohabiting couples, and couples entering marriage with children. FOCCUS can be administered individually or to a group, depending on the needs of a parish. A four-hour training session is suggested for proper administration and interpretation of the instrument.

The information that emerges from a pre-marital inventory over the course of a year in any given parish can be a helpful resource in evaluating and updating marriage preparation programs that take place in parishes, on campuses, or at the diocesan level. For more information on FOCCUS, contact the Family Life Office, Archdiocese of Omaha, 3214 N. 60th Street, Omaha, NE 68104 or call (402) 551-9003.

Chapter Three

Evangelizing the Engaged

MANY of the young couples seeking the Sacrament of Marriage are not active members of a parish community. This should come as no surprise. Many of the families seeking the sacraments of Baptism, First Communion and Confirmation are not participating in the life of their parish either. Catholic identity is sometimes more cultural than it is personal or religious. Having said that, we also want to say this: we believe that many of the young couples coming to the Church to celebrate their marriage today are wonderful people, perhaps even deeply spiritual people. They are a generation who are searching. They may be more familiar with New Age spirituality or Eastern meditation than with the Roman Catholic liturgy. It's uncommon, however, to find a young couple who view their relationship and upcoming marriage in the context of Christian faith. This presents us with a wonderful opportunity for evangelization.

In his apostolic exhortation, *On Evangelization in the Modern World,* Pope Paul VI said that evangelization is bringing the Good News of Jesus Christ into every human situation.

When are we more human than when we are falling in love, planning a wedding, a family, and a life together? These are uniquely human events that set us apart from the rest of creation. So clearly, evangelization has its place in marriage preparation. The question is, how do we go about sharing faith?

Like so many other ministries, the ministry of marriage preparation is a form of planting seeds. The soil has already been tilled, for better and for worse, by family, friends, religious background, education, and culture. We plant our seeds of faith along side the Church's seeds of sacrament, of ritual and community, and hope that somewhere along the way, young couples find the time and tools to nurture the seeds until they sprout. We begin with evangelization, sharing who we are and how the Good News of Jesus Christ has formed us and transformed us time and time again.

Dan and Kathy

Dan and Kathy were raised around the corner from one another. Their families were friendly and their brothers played on the same basketball team. Everyone was delighted when Dan and Kathy announced their engagement. But Kathy's mom had some misgivings. Dan's family were not church people. They attended Mass on Christmas and sometimes on Easter, but they didn't seem to place the same importance on religious faith as Kathy's family did.

Kathy's mom didn't want to make waves. She had known Dan's family for almost thirty years. She didn't want to appear judgmental or in any way compromise the couple's happiness. But she also felt that the difference between the way Dan and Kathy were raised would eventually become a problem in their marriage.

When Dan and Kathy went to the rectory to plan a date for their wedding, Father Ryan told them about FOCCUS and invited them to participate in marriage preparation classes. The couple set a date for FOCCUS with the Dolans, a middle aged couple who had been trained in the administration and interpretation of FOCCUS . Dan and Kathy met with them at the Dolans' home the following weekend. They completed the inventory and returned a week later to discuss their responses with them. Religious belief and practice, and the religious upbringing of their children were among the issues surfaced by FOCCUS for discussion. The Dolans facilitated a discussion about faith between Dan and Kathy. Kathy tried to explain how important it was to her that they become a couple who pray together and attend Mass together on Sundays. Dan's response was less than enthusiastic. The issue remained unresolved at the end of the FOCCUS session, but the conversation was on the table and Kathy felt happy about that. The Dolans encouraged them to continue talking about shared faith and gave them some information about Marriage Encounter and couples' workshops sponsored by their diocese. "Hold on to this, " said Mrs. Dolan. "You might want it at some point in the future."

About two months later, Dan and Kathy attended their first Pre-Cana session. The evening began with a prayer and introductions. There were eleven engaged couples, many of whom lived in the parish or had grown up in the parish and were returning to celebrate their marriage. The three presenting couples introduced themselves and gave a brief explanation as to why they were involved in the ministry of marriage preparation. Each couple, in their own way, spoke of their faith, their relationship to the Church and their desire to give something back at this point in their marriage. They talked about the role that prayer had played in their relationship, especially in the difficult times. One couple had lost a child. Another bore the burden of unemployment immediately following the birth of their fourth child. Each couple talked about weekend retreats that they had attended together and the support they felt from other couples and the clergy who they had met on those retreats.

Father Ryan spoke about his vocation to priesthood and the support that he had received from married couples through the years. He shared his struggles to remain faithful to celibacy, to prayer, and to his faith community. It was good for the engaged couples to hear that.

Dan, Kathy, and the other young couples felt as though they had been invited to share in something very special, very intimate, and very honest. This is evangelization. It's the story of lived faith. It's engaging, it's thought provoking, and by its very nature, demands some kind of response. It raises questions. Sometimes, it even raises doubt. But all these responses are a sign of a fledgling faith, a living faith, a deepening faith.

In a very unassuming way, the marriage prep team had shared the heart of who they were with the engaged couples. Later that night, as they were driving home, Dan remarked on how fervently the team had talked about the role of faith in their lives. Kathy asked him if he thought faith would ever be that important in their marriage. "If faith is connecting to people about important things like marriage and kids and problems on the job, then faith will definitely play a role in our relationship. I didn't know that's what faith was all about."

The heart of evangelization lies in relationships. The marriage prep team had been able to evangelize the engaged couples in a way that their own families could not. Dan had understood faith to be the practice of meaningless rituals. The couples, along with Father

Ryan, were able to model lived faith, and that made all the difference in Dan's own journey toward God. Kathy's mother had acted on her instincts to not interfere with the couple's relationship. As it turns out, her instincts were good ones. The door to faith was best opened by couples and clergy who were not intimately involved in the couple's future. Dan would never feel that he was coerced into religious practice by Kathy and her family, possibly putting the two families at odds. Through the team's efforts in the area of evangelization, Dan's eyes were opened in a way that he could now identify faith differently than he had in the past. There was no pressure from in-laws, no strained words exchanged. God's grace had worked through the team.

Pope John Paul II emphasized the need to meet people in the context of their lives and to speak a language that they understand. The Holy Father reminds us that people respond more to the messenger than they do to the message. The early Church grew and developed partly because the apostles were animated by the presence of God's spirit. Who we are is always much more important than what we say. If we believe that, then we know that every encounter with young couples is a form of evangelization. Whether we welcome them into our homes to talk about faith or the front page of today's newspaper, unchurched young adults are encountering the Church in you. Your hospitality, openness and friendship are the most important ingredients in proclaiming the Good News of Jesus Christ and the

Good News of Christian marriage. In you, engaged couples will come to understand what the Fathers of the Second Vatican Council meant when they used the term "domestic church" *(Gaudium et Spes, 11, 48)*. This is a concept rooted in scripture. The center of Jewish religious life was the home, particularly after the destruction of the temple in 70 A.D. Today, Jewish life is still commemorated in the home. This is where they pray over the Sabbath candles. This is where they celebrate the Passover meal.

In the late nineteenth century, Pope Leo XIII referred to the family as "the first form of the Church on earth." Your marriage and your family life can become a model of the first Church on earth for today's engaged couples. By inviting young couples into the intimacy of your home and your family life, you are inviting engaged couples to become part of your domestic church. Through your efforts and your relationship with them, they will come to understand the profound connection between their parish church and the domestic church that will be formed on their wedding day. By praying with them, you will teach them how to pray as a couple and as a community of life and love.

Chapter Four

Sharing Faith

THE evangelization that takes place in your initial meeting with engaged couples is a wonderful starting point for a process known as catechesis. The word catechesis means to hand down or echo, or in simpler terms, catechesis is the sharing of, not just our faith, but the faith of the Church, as well. It's more than the telling of our story, but the retelling of the story of Christian faith. It draws upon theology, doctrine, scripture, enculturation and the science of education. It's sharing who we are as believers, but it also explains what it is that we believe so that others can claim those beliefs as their own.

The Church believes that we're made in the image of God, and therefore, we're called be holy. In whatever way we choose to live our lives; as single individuals, as vowed religious, or as married couples, we're all called to a vocation of holiness.

Throughout history, millions upon millions of people have married, but the meaning of those marriages have varied according to the time and place in which those couples wed. For some, marriage was defined by erotic love. For others, marriage was necessary for economic survival. In some cultures, marriage takes place for the purpose of producing heirs. Marriage is a profoundly human experience involving all kinds of people in all parts of the world, but Catholics honor the marital relationship to the degree that we believe that it's also a religious sacrament. We believe that marriage is not only defined by human love, but that it's a sign or sacrament of divine love, as well. It's a way in which human beings encounter the experience of holiness. It's also a way of living out one's Christian faith in community.

Some of the young couples who come to marriage preparation are practicing Catholics with deep faith. There are others who have been raised Catholic but have drifted away from the Church. Still others come to you having had very little exposure to religious tradition after their baptism. Young couples are probably more familiar with the psychology of relationships then with the theology of marriage and family life. It's important to remember that when we begin the process of sharing faith.

Sacraments and sacraments

The heading for this section is not a typographical error. A good place to begin a discussion of marriage is to make a distinction between sacraments with a big *S* and sacraments with a little *s*. The official (big S) sacraments in the Catholic Church number seven. Little sacraments, however, are innumerable. A sacrament is, in the words of St. Augustine, "a visible sign of an invisible reality." The invisible reality is the presence and grace of God. In life, there are countless ways in which God can be revealed to the human spirit. The beauty of nature, a child's smile, an embrace, a good book or poem, a friend, or a work of art; all can open the doors to the sacred in our lives. In this sense, they are sacramental. They are visible signs of an invisible reality. They point beyond themselves to the source of all beauty and goodness, all love and truth. For Christians, the ultimate sacrament is Jesus Himself. In Christ, we believe that God has given to us the most perfect sign of Himself. Christ is the "Word made flesh," the ultimate, visible manifestation of God in our midst. Each of the seven sacraments invite us into the mystery of Christ's ongoing presence in the Church.

It seems that marriage is a sacrament in both senses of the word. Because so many of the engaged couples today are not in touch with a lived experience of faith, we can begin to help them understand marriage as a sacrament with a small s first. They understand human love. They love one another. They have probably grown as a result of that love. They have probably been challenged by that love. Their experience of human love for one another is sacramental. This is one of Christianity's most central insights about the mystery of God:

"Beloved, let us love one another because love is from God; everyone who loves is born of God and knows God. Whoever does not love does not know God, for God is love" (1 John 4:7-8).

We believe that when two people really love one another and vow to love one another forever, that love is of God whether they are Christian or not. Our first responsibility to the "unchurched" is to help them see the religious nature of their human experience.

Choosing a Church Wedding

If you ask young couples why they have decided to get married in the Church, you will probably hear the following:

"I'm a Catholic and Catholics get married in a church."

"It would break my mother's heart if I didn't."

"It's much more beautiful in a church. The pictures come out great."

"My faith is very important to me and I want the Eucharist to be part of my marriage."

"It makes sense to invite God to be a part of the biggest day of our lives."

"It's important to my spouse."

The responses will range from the sublime to the ridiculous. Now is the time to help them appreciate why Catholics think getting married in church is important and meaningful. At the heart of the matter is the fact that the Church is not a building. The Church is a community of believers. It is people of faith. The church building is where the Church often meets for prayer and worship. The building has no real meaning apart from the community of faith. We celebrate marriage in a church building because it is the sacred space of the community. It's the Spirit of God alive in the community that sanctifies the space. To be married in a church building when we have no connection to the community makes little sense. Marriage provides the opportunity for a couple to celebrate their connection to the Catholic community or at least to re-evaluate it. Couples should be challenged to recognize the meaning of getting married in the Church. Marriage in the Church is an expression, not only of love, but of faith. When couples marry in the Church, they invite Christ into their marriage. They not only celebrate the Sacrament of Marriage, they become the sacrament.

Living the Sacrament

The Church names marriage as one of the sacraments of vocation (the other being Holy Orders). A married couple becomes a walking, talking, breathing sign of God's love in the world. Marriage is a sacrament that cannot be left at the altar but must be lived daily. Christian marriage is a sign of God's indissoluble love. Is there anything that you can do that would cause God to turn His back on you? Of course not. God's love for us is unconditional and eternal. Likewise, marriage is a sign of God's indissoluble, eternal love. Shakespeare wrote, "love is not love which alters when it alteration finds, or bends with the remover to remove. Oh no, it is an ever-fixed mark that looks on tempests and cannot be shaken."

Marriage is a commitment to another human being, one who will grow and change through the years. Christian marriage promises love throughout life's many changes. This is not an idea that our culture supports strongly, but it is the very heart of a sacramental marriage. At the time of Christ, Jewish law allowed a man to divorce his wife by giving her a written decree. Jesus insisted that marriage was forever. He defined marriage as more than a human arrangement. It's a sacred bond. "Therefore, what God has joined together, let no one separate" (Matthew 19:6). The heart and soul of Christian marriage is the wedding vow. Couples minister the sacrament to each other through their vows. The priest or deacon is simply the witness. It's the vow to love each other forever that forms the bond of the sacrament. (Note: The church allows for a marriage to be annulled in cases where one or both of the spouses were not truly free to make a commitment to marriage. If a person is psychologically incapable of the marital commitment, their vows are, unfortunately, empty).

The Sacrament of Marriage is sign of God's intimate love. In marriage, the two shall be as one. In marriage there is an emotional, psychological and physical union which is unique to wedded love. The intimate love of marriage means that we come to know a person with all their strengths and weaknesses and love them as they are. Real intimacy is only achieved after a certain period of disillusionment when we discover that the beloved is not exactly who we thought they were. Real intimacy is a commitment to unconditional love for the beloved. It involves the willingness to let go of masks and defenses and be ourselves. It involves a profound trust in the love of another human being. Through this love, we see signs of God's intimate and unconditional love for us.

Christian marriage is a reminder of the Incarnation. Christians believe that God took on flesh in the person of Jesus. More than anywhere else, we encounter the sacred in other human beings. Every human being is, in some sense, a mini-incarnation, a sign of God's presence on earth. For a married couple, the path to God must go in and through their spouse. Marriage is a reminder that we believe in a God who does not live up in the clouds but is present most deeply in human beings.

Christian marriage is a call to community. The followers of Jesus have always believed that Christ lives on in and through the Spirit in community.

Christianity is not about "me and God" it's about "us and God." Marriage as a sacrament is a call to live as a part of a community of faith. The family will become a "domestic church" which will extend outward to the parish and the universal church. Marriage is our first community of life and love, sharing itself with the larger community of faith where the values of the gospel are nurtured and lived.

Christian marriage involves dying and rising with Christ. It can be a sign of Christ's suffering and redemptive love. It's an invitation to share not only friendship, affection, and sexual love, but to love one another through life's most difficult times. In marriage, we help carry each other through sickness and sorrow. We suffer with each other and lay down our lives for one another. The cross is not a stranger to couples who share in Christian marriage. In St. Paul's words, we are called to "bear one another's burdens; and in this way you will fulfill the law of Christ" (Galatians 6:2). Christians are continually called to grow, to live and die and rise with Christ. In that way, the mystery of marriage mirrors the Paschal Mystery.

The marriage of our twenties died and gave rise to the new concerns and responsibilities of our thirties and forties. Middle age and old age will bring with them new challenges and new love, a deeper, more mature love. Conflict, alienation, forgiveness, and reconciliation mirror the death and resurrection of Jesus Christ. The greatest power that we have as a couple is the power to love new life into each other. We're called time and again to love our marriages back to life. There may be times when we feel like we are standing beside the tomb of a dead marriage. All of our best efforts seem to be failing. Marriage involves an act of faith that God has brought you together and He will not abandon you in the difficulties of your marriage.

Christian marriage is supported by prayer. Just as the Church has its prayers and rituals, so too, the domestic church has its prayers and patterns of celebration and reconciliation. Each domestic church has its sacraments, the ways in which they love one another and discover God in their marriage and family life. Every domestic church has its holy days; the couple's wedding anniversary, the birth dates of their children. The celebration of these days and the many sacramental moments of marriage, serve to support the couple in their journey toward God. If marriage is an act of faith as well as an act of love, then it would seem natural to nurture that marriage with prayer. Prayer helps couples to transcend their differences and to root their lives in God's unconditional love. Prayer invites them to recognize Christ as the invisible partner in their marriage. Prayer is an invitation to let go of selfishness and bitterness and clothe ourselves in love and mercy. Couples who can pray together root their marriage in something bigger than themselves.

The Sacrament of Marriage is renewed in the Sacrament of the Eucharist. Catholics renew and cele-

brate their faith each Sunday at Mass. For married couples, the Eucharist is an invitation to live their sacrament more deeply. It's a special time when the two
shall be one in faith and love and in the Body of Christ.

Christian marriage is a call to discipleship.
Marriages that are rooted in faith will look different
than other marriages. Nearly all married couples want
happiness, financial security, healthy, happy children.
They seek opportunities for personal growth and
leisure time for re-creation. Those are normal human
goals. Christians can want those things, too. But they
also long for more. Christian marriages are in some
ways counter-cultural. They can't bow before celebrity
and money and power. Christian marriages are called
to live for God's kingdom and not their own. In
Christian marriages, we find couples whose lives
embrace service to others and a commitment to those
most in need.

A Living Faith

In order to help young couples understand the relationship between faith and marriage, we need to be
clear on the connection that the two have in our lives.
In the Catholic tradition, faith has many distinct dimensions. The affective dimension of faith is our personal
relationship with God. It is the connection between
ourselves and God that flows from the heart and
involves trust, love, awe, and wonder, as well as doubt,
fear and sometimes confusion. The intellectual or cog-

nitive dimension of faith is expressed in the creeds, doctrine, and theology. On this level, faith involves an openness to God's truth and a genuine desire to understand that truth. Faith is also something that we live. If it is limited to our personal relationship with God and what we believe, but is never evident in our relationships to others, it's basically dead faith. Our faith must be translated into action because ours is a communal faith as well as a personal faith. It is not my faith alone. It is our faith together. It is deeply personal, but it's not private. Our Christian faith challenges us to live in the service of the Kingdom of God.

Years ago, we studied at the Institute of Religious Education and Pastoral Ministry at Boston College. It was there we were introduced to Tom Groome and his groundbreaking method of catechesis. We've found it to be particularly helpful in sharing faith with engaged couples. Groome suggests that religious education should involve both self-discovery and insight into an ongoing religious tradition. Its goal is not simply to communicate information, but to draw people toward conversion. This conversion is a way of looking at life through the gospel. It involves a conscious commitment to living for God's kingdom, rather than our own. It takes place in the context of a Christian community which has both a past to be conserved and a future to be realized. It calls people to personal freedom and social justice. Groome lists five "steps" in sharing faith. They're meant to invite people to get in touch with their present experience of faith, to understand the roots of that experience, to view it in light of the Church's story and vision, and to imagine new and richer ways of living our faith.

Step One: Naming present action

The first step invites the participants to articulate for themselves their present level of lived faith. Remember, "evangelization is the starting point for ministry, the recognition of the presence of God already in young people, their experiences, their families, and their culture. Evangelization, therefore, enables young adults to uncover and name the experience of God already active and present in their lives" (*Renewing the Vision: A Framework for Catholic Youth Ministry*, NCCB/USCC, 1997).

We should keep in mind that our goal is to help the engaged couples nurture their present faith and not to judge their worthiness for marriage in the Church. In other words, we should clearly convey an attitude of respect and nonjudgment. You might want to begin by asking the couples to respond to some of the following questions:

- Where are you in terms of the Church and religious faith?
- Do you go to church?
- Why or why not?
- Do you belong to a parish?
- When do you pray?

• Do you pray together?

• Do you feel as if you have a relationship with God?

• What is your image of God?

• Do you see any connection between your faith and your marriage?

These questions should be personal, not intellectual. Faith, like marriage, is a journey involving the heart, mind, and the quality of our relationships with others. Hopefully, each couple discovers this in time.

Step Two: The participants' stories and visions

The purpose of the second step is to help young couples to understand the roots of their present level of lived faith and to examine where this will lead them in the future. This process could be facilitated with the following questions:

• What type of religious upbringing did you have?

• What do you think were its strengths and weaknesses?

• Who has had the most influence on your faith?

• Are you satisfied with your present level of faith?

• Are you interested in growing spiritually?

• How can the Sacrament of Marriage nurture your faith?

• How would you like to see your children grow in faith?

• How will you introduce your children to God?

• How will you help them grow in relationship to their Creator?

Step Three: Sharing the story and vision of Christian faith

The third step involves education. Here is where we communicate information. This is where we describe the Church's understanding of the relationship between faith and marriage. The Christian "story" includes the ways in which we have understood marriage in our faith tradition. The Christian "vision" refers to ways in which we can imagine the Sacrament of Marriage as it is lived personally and in society. Christians understand marriage not only as an act of love, but an act of faith as well. St. John writes that God is love, and therefore, we see the Sacrament of Marriage as a door to the sacred. In faith, we are committed to living our married lives in the context of a Christian community. Beyond that, as followers of Jesus Christ we are committed to lives of service, especially to those who are most in need. The ideal here is to communicate an understanding of marriage as a sacrament without using theological jargon with which most young couples are unfamiliar. We've found it helpful to share some of our own experiences of faith with young couples; what it looked like when we were dating and how it's changed through the years. Don't be afraid to share your own story of faith, warts and all.

Pat and Tony

When we were dating, we made it a point to pray together. We attended Mass together and

took time away from our jobs and families to par-
ticipate in a weekend retreat experience for
Catholic couples. We also sought opportunities
for religious education. We read books on theolo-
gy and spirituality and we attended lectures that
were sponsored by Catholic universities or local
parishes. We somehow understood that as our
lives changed, so too, our faith deepened.

As we moved from seeing ourselves as two sep-
arate individuals toward understanding ourselves
as a couple, our faith seemed to change to accom-
modate the gift of love to and from one another.
Of course, nothing changed us more profoundly
than the birth of our first child. The experience of
parenthood expanded our love, our faith, and our
gratitude for life.

We had always prayed together before meals.
When Christine was born, she sat between us in
her infant seat, and later in her high chair while
we prayed. We made a point of holding her hand
and each other's while we gave thanks for our
food and for each other.

One evening, when Christine was about eight
months old, we had an argument while preparing
dinner. When dinner was ready, we set the table,
sat down and began to eat. We were both too
angry to join hands and pray. As we lifted our
forks, Christine must have noticed that we forgot
something. Sitting in her high chair between us,

she extended her hands to both of us. At 8 months of age, Christine was calling us to prayer. The catechesis that had taken place in our home had taken root in our child, and she was now able to catechize us. Faith changes everything.

Step Four: Dialogue

The couples are invited to reflect on their experience in light of Christian faith and to reflect on Christian faith in light of their experience. The result will likely involve a critique of both. Participants should have the opportunity to reflect on the Christian view of marriage whether or not they decide to embrace it as their own.

• Are you willing to live out your vocation to Christian marriage in the context of a community of faith?

• Can you make a commitment to serving others?

• Are you open to the experience of shared prayer?

• Will your marriage ceremony reflect your faith as well as your love?

The engaged couples should be invited to respond to the Church's lived experience of faith. This is not meant to simply be a "gripe session," but an authentic way of looking at how the Church could improve its lived faith, as well. For example, one might ask them what kind of support and enrichment is available for married couples within their local parish or diocese. It would be a good idea to have information on hand about programs in your area that are available to newlyweds or married couples. In addition, participants might want to raise other issues of faith that are troubling to them. The focus of this step is not giving final answers or winning a debate, but merely providing the time and space for listening and dialogue.

Step Five: Conclusions and decisions

Lastly, the couples are invited to begin drawing conclusions in light of the process that has just taken place. Of course, these conclusions must be freely chosen. Perhaps some will reacquaint themselves with their parish or try to renew their commitment to the Eucharist. Others might simply decide to learn more about their faith or to discuss it more as a couple. A list of affordable, contemporary books can be provided. Some couples might make a decision to pray together regularly. Still others may find a way that they can become involved in some form of community service. The final step asks each couple to consider what they will do differently as a result of having participated in this process. Pope John Paul II reminds us in his apostolic letter, *On the Family*, that the very preparation for Christian marriage is itself a journey of faith. It is a special opportunity for the engaged to rediscover and deepen the faith received in baptism and nourished by their Christian upbringing. It's a time when the Word made Flesh is transformed into the Word made fresh for a new generation of Christian families. It's hopefully a time when each couple comes to recognize and freely accept their vocation to serve the kingdom of God as a married couple.

Chapter Five

A Family Perspective

IN 1987, the NCCB Ad Hoc Committee on Marriage and Family Life published a manual for all pastoral leaders entitled *A Family Perspective in Church and Society.* It called the Church to reflect on its own vision of family life and to extend its hospitality to families of all kinds.

Family life continues to evolve in the third millennium, presenting people involved in ministry with a unique set of challenges. It's important to remember that the engaged couples with whom we come in contact are coming from diverse backgrounds, each with their own developmental history. The Committee on Marriage and Family Life included in its manual an overview of the family life cycle, an important perspective in understanding and ministering effectively to families today. At each stage of development, a family and each of its members must address issues of cohesion and adaptability. No time is that more evident than when a child, and often today, a parent, moves toward a new marriage and the creation of a new family. The family life cycle stages have been identified as:

Establishment: a time for a newly married couple to become a separate, but connected unit of their extended family systems.

New parents: when a couple or a single adult establishes a new family consisting of their own parent-child relationships.

School age family: how the couple or single parent with school age children and adolescents fosters individuation and the growth of each member of the family, redefining family participation.

Empty nest family: when children leave home and the couple or single parent is alone, family members must regroup and relate to one another (and in-laws) on an adult-to-adult level.

Aging family: how the couple or single adult after retirement begins to deal with issues of illness, death, role reversals and diminishing resources.

Of course, divorce and remarriage and the birth of children in a second or third marriage must be considered in today's families. Blended families are commonplace as are children being born to unmarried women. One third of all children born in the United States are born to single women. These developments in family life all hold their own joys and challenges.

Members of the marriage prep team will no doubt come in contact with all kinds of family situations. We found it helpful to use the family life cycle as a way to approach ministry with families. Although the ministry of marriage preparation deals most directly with the

engaged couple, a family perspective is always necessary if we are to help the engaged couple understand
their families of origin and the impact that their family
life has had, and will continue to have, on their lives.

The Family of Origin

If the truth be told, a couple's introduction to marriage preparation doesn't really take place in a parish
or diocesan program, but in their families of origin.
John Paul II, in his apostolic exhortation, *On the
Family,* called this *remote marriage preparation.* Each
bride and groom approach the altar with twenty to thirty years of preparation for marriage—all the things
they learned as they watched their parents' marriages
grow and deepen, or in some cases, dissolve. Most of
what they know about love, commitment, communication, emotion, affection, bonding, separation, parenting, money, and faith has been learned, for better or for
worse, in the home in which they grew up. Unfortunately, in some cases, everything that they know about
addiction, co-dependency, and domestic violence has
also been learned in their families of origin.

Present day marriage prep programs recognize that
each bride and groom-to-be make their way toward
marriage with individual histories and unique genetic
constitutions. With a better informed understanding of
human development, marriage preparation programs
recognize that they are not providing couples with their
first experience of preparation for marriage, but rather,

an opportunity for engaged couples to accurately interpret the years of preparation that have already taken place. The Holy Father refers to this process as the *immediate preparation* for the sacrament of Marriage.

The priests and deacons, religious and lay couples who comprise the marriage prep teams are welcoming engaged couples into a process in which they can begin to examine the familial relationships that were critical to their development and ultimately, to the development of the family life that they will create when they marry. The Church can provide engaged couples with the information and encouragement needed to look honestly and objectively at their personal histories within the context of faith and in the presence of God's healing love. We can assist the couples in identifying the roles that they played in their families of origin and how this will influence the way in which they accept their roles as husband and wife when they marry. Hopefully this endeavor will move the couple toward a deeper appreciation of the many gifts that they received from their parents and extended family members. Perhaps it will help them grow in their recognition of the fact that some aspects of their childhood were less than perfect, perhaps even detrimental to the formation of a healthy marriage. As mentioned in a previous chapter, FOCCUS can be very helpful, along with the support and guidance of marriage preparation ministers, in moving the engaged couple toward the recognition, and in some cases, the resolution of some of the issues that existed, and perhaps still exist, in their families of origin. Occasionally, members of the marriage preparation team may be called to act as advocates for the engaged couple as they seek to become independent of the family dynamics that could be preventing them from freely choosing to marry. An unexpected pregnancy is sometimes the reason that families encourage a young couple to marry, less so today than in years gone by, but occasionally that thinking prevails. In a situation such as this, the priest, deacon or sponsor couple may have to advocate on behalf of the young couple. A family perspective is critical to the resolution of a sensitive situation such as this.

Many of the marriage preparation programs that have been developed in recent years have been updated to include information about the impact of the family of origin on personality development and life choices. Newer programs also include the research emerging from the empirical sciences on genetics and biochemistry and the role they play in addiction, codependency, depression, anxiety, abuse, and other issues that we now know with certainty can contribute to divorce. These programs place more emphasis on family systems, conflict resolution skills, personality types and differences, as well as biological predispositions toward personality disorders and mood disorders that increase the likelihood that maladaptive behaviors will be repeated from generation to generation.

Today, we are fortunate to have the insights of science, often popularized by authors such as Judith

Wallerstein and her colleagues. They have spent 25 years studying the long term effects of marriage and divorce on children. They followed youngsters, whose parents had divorced, into adult life. Their most recent book, *The Unexpected Legacy of Divorce,* explores the impact of divorce on a generation of children who grew up with parents who chose divorce more often than any other generation before them. Wallerstein and her colleagues surface some helpful insights into the legacy of divorce and the ways in which it continues to shape the lives of young adults today.

What does this have to do with preparing a couple to celebrate a sacrament? St. Aquinas said grace builds on nature. We need to look at our human nature, our tendencies, both inherited and environmental, that contribute to the way that we think and behave. The more clearly that we understand our humanity, the more deeply we can begin to understand how God's grace works to call us to share in the life of Christ, both human and divine.

In addition to revising the programs and printed materials used to prepare young couples for marriage, Church leaders have carefully designed formation programs to address the spiritual development and ministerial training of marriage preparation ministers; the priests, deacons, religious, and lay couples who give so much of themselves to the couples preparing for marriage. Being an effective minister requires more than a desire to serve others. Ministry demands a deepening knowledge of self, of God, and the people who form faith communities.

The Office of Pastoral Formation in the Diocese of Rockville Centre is one of many offices offering a formation program for priests, deacons, and lay couples involved in the ministry of marriage preparation. An important component of the program consists in studying the family of origin, family systems, family dynamics, communication, and the family life cycle. In addition, training in the administration and interpretation of pre-marital inventories such as FOCCUS is provided regularly. Sessions can be offered in a variety of ways in order to accommodate the busy schedules of those who are involved in ministry today. For more information regarding the formation of marriage preparation ministers, contact Sister Lauren Hanley, Director of the Office of Pastoral Formation, (516) 678-5800, ext. 539.

Chapter Six

Cohabitation

JOE and Jenny dated two years before they decided
to live together. After a year of cohabiting, Joe and
Jenny decided to get married. The fact is, the majority
of couples in the United States live together before they
get married, presenting the Church with a sensitive
pastoral dilemma. How can we respond effectively to a
cohabiting couple and at the same time remain faithful
to our understanding of the Sacrament of Marriage?
Perhaps the answer lies in the words of St. Francis of
Assisi, who prayed to "seek first to understand, then to
be understood."

Our best efforts to understand cohabiting couples
may be only guesses. Cohabitation could be sympto-
matic of the tenuous manner in which Americans view
relationships and commitment. A couple who decide to
live together could be saying that a childhood filled
with fragmented families and fluctuating values has
left them with serious concerns about their ability to
love and be loved forever.

Cohabitation could be an attempt at "safe love," but
like "safe sex," its a contradiction in terms. Sex isn't
safe. Neither is love. Both involve self-gift, vulnerabili-

ty, and trust. Both beg commitment because they are fraught with the life-giving grace of God. Living together, a decision that could be wrapped in hesitation and anxiety, is a half-hearted arrangement with serious consequences.

Contrary to popular belief that living together is safer than marriage in some respects, research indicates that cohabiting relationships are much more likely to end than marriages, and end badly. Young men and women walk away (or limp away) from these relationships feeling that they cannot trust their partners or their own judgment in choosing a mate. Some recent studies show that even one failed cohabiting relationship can negatively impact the level of trust, health, and happiness of future relationships, including marriage. Paradoxically, in trying to create situations in which couples can protect themselves from the trappings of marriage, they place themselves at greater risk and unknowingly set the stage for emotional, psychological, and spiritual disaster.

If the ecclesial community can gain a more nuanced understanding of the many factors that impact a couple's decision to live together, perhaps we would be better prepared to meet the unique ministerial needs that the cohabiting couple brings with them when they approach the Church to celebrate their marriage. The National Conference of Catholic Bishops explored new ways to effectively minister to an ever-evolving Catholic community. In 1996, they released a document entitled, *Sons and Daughters of the Light: A National Pastoral Plan for Ministry with Young Adults,* in which the bishops encouraged a pastoral approach toward cohabiting couples that is welcoming and without judgment. They warned that a confrontation or condemnation of the cohabiting couple could be taken as rejection, crippling those who are trying to respond to the call of Christian marriage. Using terms such as "living in sin" can risk further alienation of those who are already marginal Catholics. Pope John Paul II recommends that pastors and pastoral leaders make "tactful and respectful" contact with cohabiting couples, witnessing Christian family life in such a way as to smooth the path for them to embrace the sacrament of Marriage.

The ministerial challenge and catechetical demands facing couples and clergy involved in marriage preparation today are daunting. They are asked to continually gain a deeper and more compassionate understanding of a wide range of variables that impact a couple's decision to live together before marriage. Pastoral experience has made it clear that cohabitation is understood differently in cultures outside our own. Young people fleeing the problems of the third world often cohabit and have families outside of Christian marriage. Some couples choose to live together for economic reasons and others for reasons of personal safety. It's also important to remember that couples who cohabit for the first time after becoming engaged seem to escape the disastrous effects of cohabitation that have impacted the majority of cohabiting couples.

Despite their history and individual reasons for living together, cohabiting couples are approaching the Church to celebrate their love for one another in the midst of a faith-filled community. Let's invite them into the celebration of the life of the Church, the sacraments, and the living Word of God. Let's offer them the support that a life-giving community can provide in critical times of transition. Let's invite them to share in the process of evangelization where they come to recognize Christ and gospel values in their lives, their choices, and in their love for one another. This process should encourage couples to examine the reasons why they chose to live together and ask them to explore their patterns of communication and decision making in the eyes of a compassionate God. If we challenge them in a manner that is non-threatening, in the spirit of charity and humility, perhaps we can help to foster self-awareness and strengthen their relationship to each other, to the Church, and ultimately to Christ.

The United States Bishops Committee on Marriage and Family has prepared a report called "Marriage Preparation and Cohabiting Couples." It is one of the most comprehensive documents on cohabitation to date. The report is not considered an official statement of the NCCB/USCC, but was published as a resource paper offering sociological data as well as reflection on the religious questions surrounding cohabitation. Part

I of the report includes the following information about cohabitation:

- The number of cohabiting couples has risen consistently in the past thirty years.

- More than half of all first marriages in the United States today are preceded by cohabitation. Clearly, there has been a declining significance of marriage as the foundation of family life in the United States. Milestones once associated with marriage, such as sexual intimacy, childbearing, and establishing a home now occur without a wedding.

- Cohabitation is experienced as an alternative to marriage or an attempt to prepare for marriage. About 30 percent of cohabitors never intend to marry. Twenty percent of cohabitors disagree on whether or not they intend to marry. Less than half of cohabiting couples ever marry.

- Cohabiting couples who do marry are twice as likely to divorce as couples who did not cohabit prior to marriage.

- Most marriages that were preceded by cohabitation end in divorce within the early years of marriage, however, after seven years of marriage, marital stability for both those who cohabited before marriage and those who didn't, levels out.

- Those who cohabit more than once before they marry have higher divorce rates than those who only had one cohabiting relationship before marriage.

- Median duration for cohabitation is 1.3 years.

- The divorce rate is higher for those who cohabit more than three years prior to marriage.

- Women are likely to cohabit only once, and this tends to be with the man they subsequently marry. Men are more likely to cohabit with a series of partners.

- Individuals, particularly females, who experienced marital disruption in their family of origin, are more likely to cohabit than those who were raised by parents who enjoyed a stable marriage.

- College graduates are less likely to cohabit than high school graduates.

- Individuals who cohabit tend to value independence more than interdependence. Couples who did not cohabit prior to marriage tend to place more value on interdependence in marriage.

- Couples who cohabit before marriage have more conflict over money than couples who did not cohabit before marriage. Set patterns of autonomy or competition surrounding the earning and handling of money in the cohabiting relationship tend to carry over into marriage, particularly if the couple has not discussed marital finances before marriage.

- Cohabiting couples have less effective conflict resolution skills than couples who marry without first cohabiting. A cohabiting couple may have a greater fear of upsetting an uncommitted relationship or less investment in protecting a temporary relationship. Patterns of communication are often carried over from cohabitation to marriage.

• Domestic violence is more common in cohabitation than in marriage and is more likely to exist in a marriage that was preceded by cohabitation.

• A woman who cohabited before marriage is 3.3 times more likely to be unfaithful to her husband than a woman who did not cohabit before marriage.

• Forty percent of cohabiting households include children, either the children of the cohabiting relationship or children that one or both partners brought to the cohabiting relationship.

• Individuals who regard religious participation as unimportant are more likely to cohabit than those who practice a religious faith.

• Individuals who cohabit tend to be more liberal and more risk-oriented than those who did not cohabit before marriage.

The reasons individuals give for cohabitation include the following:

• Fear of long-term commitment
• Desire to avoid divorce
• Desire for economic security
• Escape from family of origin
• Transition to adulthood
• Desire to test the relationship
• Pressure to conform to the cultural norm of cohabitation
• Desire for stability in raising children
• Rejection of the institution of marriage

Part II of the Committee's report discusses the pastoral issues that should be raised with cohabiting couples who decide to marry in the Church. The recommendations are preceded by the recognition that adolescence is a more appropriate time to raise issues of chastity, fidelity, and the meaning of marriage as a sacrament. High school and college students can be catechized in a way that enables them to make informed, faith-filled and life-giving choices throughout their lives.

The Committee acknowledges the reality that most couples preparing for the Sacrament of Marriage are presently cohabiting. Pastoral leaders have identified cohabitation as one of the most difficult issues to be raised in marriage preparation. The Committee offers the following suggestions in the hope of providing guidance to priests, deacons, and lay couples as they prepare cohabiting couples for Christian marriage:

• The factors that lead a couple into cohabitation can include difficult economic, cultural or religious situations, extreme ignorance or poverty, or psychological immaturity. The ecclesial community should take care to become acquainted with each situation, case by case.

• Each contact with the cohabiting couple should be respectful. Care should be taken to avoid immediately confronting the couple or condemning their behavior.

• Marriage preparation is an opportunity for evangelization and catechesis. The cohabiting couple should be welcomed with the gospel and at the same time challenged by its message of commitment and faithfulness.

• A pre-marital inventory such as FOCCUS can surface the issue of cohabitation comfortably and early in the marriage preparation process. Cohabitation should not be ignored. A straightforward attitude can encourage the couple to reflect on their decision to cohabit so that they gain insight into the their relationship and the consequences of their living arrangement.

• Marriage preparation presents a "teachable moment." The time should be taken to enlighten couples patiently and charitably.

• The faith community should witness Christian family life in a way that the couple can work through the challenges of having cohabited before marriage and be drawn more deeply into the life of the Church and their vocation to Christian marriage.

• The cohabiting couple can be encouraged to live chastely before marriage once the Church's teaching on marriage and sexuality is carefully explained, but a pastoral minister should know the particular circumstances of the couple's relationship, e.g., Are children living with the couple? Are there safety issues that need to be considered? and advise the couple accordingly.

• Cohabitation is not in itself a canonical impediment to marriage, therefore, the couple cannot be refused marriage solely on the basis of their living situation.

• The celebration of the Sacrament of Reconciliation should be encouraged for all couples as part of
the marriage preparation process.

• Canon Law provides no special consideration for
the weddings of cohabiting couples. Every couple is
entitled to a fruitful liturgical celebration of marriage in
which the spouses share in the mystery of unity and the
fruitful love that exists between Christ and the Church.

The full report can be downloaded from the
NCCB/USCC Website at www.nccbuscc.org or ordered
by phone at 1-800-235-8722.

Chapter Seven

Great Sex

WHAT makes great sex? We can't answer that for everyone, but it's a great icebreaker for a session on sexuality with engaged couples. Let's face it, sex is probably one of the most powerful and pleasurable parts of their relationship. I'm sure the topic would hold their attention, unless we lose them in the first moments with a lot of rules.

What makes great sex is a question whose answer will be impacted by the culture in which we live, the religious formation that we've had, and our experiences of our own sexuality. If this is true, then this question will have many answers, depending on the personal histories of the people answering the question.

It's probably a good idea to begin a discussion on sexuality with an admission of humility. Human sexuality is not a topic that has a clear beginning, middle, and end; nor is it a question that has one correct answer. Anyone who has sexuality neatly packed away as a question that's been asked and answered probably shouldn't be trusted.

Our sexuality is a central, vital, changing, challenging, joyous, confusing, and remarkable part of who we are. Our understanding of our own sexuality and human sexuality is a mysterious journey. The Church walks with us on this journey. At the second Vatican Council, the Church asserted that "the joys and the hopes, the griefs and anxieties, of the men and women of this age. . . . these too are the joys and hopes, griefs and anxieties of the followers of Christ" (*Gaudium et spes*, no.1).

It would be a mistake to assume that the Church has come to a conclusion, and therefore, stopped examining, the many ways in which our humanity is lived out. The Church recognizes the complexities of humanity, and certainly of human sexuality. Like the rest of the world: the scientists, psychologists, artists, couples, and individuals who continue to explore the many meanings of human sexuality; the Church continues to grow in its understanding of this wondrous part of our humanity, as well. And that might surprise a lot of people, particularly the young couples getting married today.

The Catholic Church gains its understanding of human sexuality from natural law, Scripture, human experience, and the information that continues to emerge from empirical studies.

Together, these disciplines have influenced the Church's teaching on sexuality today. The Second Vatican Council spoke of humanity in holistic terms, and in doing so, renewed our understanding of our sexuality as an integral part of our being, not just our physical existence, but our spirituality, as well.

Sexuality is not so much sexual activity as it is a human way of being present to God and one another. We relate as sexual persons. At no time are we living and loving apart from our sexuality. Human sexuality is not a biological function of our personalities, it is a manifestation of who we are, the way we live and respond to the world around us. It is the way we grow and develop intrapersonally and interpersonally. Human sexuality is not simply about procreation. If that were true, then like animals, we would not become sexually aroused outside of our fertile periods. The Church believes that our sexuality is more than procreative. It is relational. It helps us bond and deepen our capacity to love and be one with another. In that way, our sexuality is an important element in our spirituality. Human beings make love, which is much more than having sex. Human beings are the only species that face one another during intercourse. We make eye contact, we communicate deep feelings when making love. For human beings, sex involves much more than our bodies. It's the work of the spirit, as well.

Our sexuality opens us to a more profound understanding of the Incarnation. This is the teaching that is embraced by the Church today. Surely, we can gain some insight into the scriptural understanding of sexuality, in both the Old and New Testaments, but remember, the Bible was written in a time when people were put to death for adultery and homosexual acts, a time when fathers sold their daughters, and men could divorce a woman on a whim. Today, we glean new insights into the scriptural stories of human sexuality.

The book of Genesis contains two different accounts of Creation. In the first account, God creates the world in six days and rests on the seventh. It was on the sixth day that God created human beings.

"Then God said: 'Let us make human beings in our image, after our likeness, to have dominion over the fish in the sea, the birds of the air, and the cattle . . . God created human beings in his own image; in the image of God he created them; male and female he created them. God blessed them, and God said to them, 'Be fruitful and multiply, and fill the earth and subdue it; and have dominion over the fish of the sea and over the birds of the air and over every living thing that moves upon the earth.' . . . And it was so. God saw everything that he had made, and indeed, it was very good" (Genesis 1:26-31).

The author of this Creation account is onto something profoundly important. First, we are created in the image of God. (The word "man" means human being, not male). It is specifically as male and female that we are created in the image of God. Although, we traditionally speak of God in masculine language, God's image is found in the complimentarity of our maleness and our femaleness. Sexuality is created by God so that Creation can share in God's creative power: "Be fertile and multiply, fill the earth." The procreative dimension to human sexuality is perceived as part of God's purpose in creating a differentiation of the sexes.

If the story of Creation ended here, human sexuality would not be intended to be different from animal sexuality. Sex keeps the species going. But the second account of Creation reveals a more complex understanding of the mystery of our sexuality. In this story, the man has been created from clay and has been given every good thing in the garden of Eden. But it's not enough.

"Then the Lord God said, 'It is not good that the man should be alone; I will make him a helper as his partner.' . . . So the Lord God caused a deep sleep to fall upon the man, and he slept; then he took one of his ribs and closed up its place with flesh. And the rib that the Lord God had taken from the man he made into a woman and brought her to the man. And then the man said, 'This at last is bone of my bones and flesh of my flesh; this one shall be called Woman, for out of Man this one was taken.' Therefore a man leaves his father and mother and clings to his wife, and they become one flesh. And the man and his wife were both naked, and were not ashamed" (Genesis 2:18-25).

In this story, we find a more "psychological" understanding of sexuality. The man and the woman are suitable partners. They are to become "one body" in a relationship that will be more important than one's relationship to any other creature, more important than one's relationship to one's mother and father. They are naked with one another and feel no shame. The writer seems to convey a personal as well as a physical nakedness where nothing stands between them. Our sexuality has been created for intimacy and union. Marriage, in some ways, is a return to Eden, a time and place when a man and a woman came together in nakedness. This is reflected in their bodies and their entire selves. Being physically naked fits the nature of the relationship because they are to have no barriers between them.

But the story of Adam and Eve doesn't end here. There were problems in Paradise. Adam and Eve sinned. Their sin came between them and between God. They were then ashamed of their nakedness. They covered themselves in fig leaves. Well, today, couples don't don themselves in fig leaves, but they still lose their "nakedness" with each other. They still sin, they destroy trust and harmony and begin to clothe themselves in all types of emotional or material fig leaves. And before they know it, great sex is a distant memory.

Tim and MaryEllen

Tim and MaryEllen met in college and dated throughout senior year. After graduation, Tim found a job in New York and MaryEllen began teaching in Philadelphia. They traveled to see each other on weekends for almost two years. They decided to marry as soon as MaryEllen finished her Master's degree.

After the wedding, MaryEllen moved to New York. Their marriage seemed nearly perfect. They enjoyed a warm and wonderful sexual relationship in which they both found much pleasure and affirmation. They planned romantic evenings at home and time with friends and family on the weekends.

Tim loved his job on Wall Street. MaryEllen wanted to teach kindergarten, as she had in Philadelphia, but had difficulty finding a job in New York. Tim worked long hours and rarely made it home for dinner, but MaryEllen met him in the city whenever she could and together they planned a night at the theater or a weekend getaway where they could spend some time alone.

When MaryEllen found a job teaching third grade in White Plains, she began to spend much of her time preparing lessons to meet the requirements of a demanding curriculum with which she was unfamiliar. Even her weekends were consumed with catching up and getting ready for the coming week. Tim and MaryEllen spent fewer hours with each other and often she was asleep before he got home at night. Their sexual rela-

tionship was not what it was in the first few months of their marriage. Neither was their emotional relationship.

Changes at Tim's firm required more hours. He knew MaryEllen would be working on her lesson plans or already asleep when he got home, so he often had dinner with colleagues or met friends from college after work. When their first wedding anniversary rolled around, they felt that they were different people. They were not as connected emotionally or sexually as they had been in the months following their wedding. They talked about the changes that had taken place in their relationship and in their careers. They decided to alter their schedules so that they were free to spend every Sunday together, an idea that would have helped nurture their relationship if Tim's father hadn't had a stroke later that month. Shortly after the stroke, Tim and MaryEllen received a letter from their landlord saying that the house that they were renting was being sold and they would have to move within the next two months. They had talked about buying a house in the next few years, and felt this was probably the time to start looking to purchase a home rather than renting another apartment. The following month, Tim was offered a promotion that would require some traveling. The increase in salary would help them with the down payment for a home, but the traveling would cut into the week-ends. They would have fewer hours together than ever before.

The stroke suffered by Tim's father had left him completely paralyzed on his right side. Tim's mother looked to Tim and MaryEllen for help. They wanted to help, but they felt that they were being pulled in too many directions. Leisure time seemed to be a thing of the past and their sexual relationship became stale. Intimacy, both emo-tional and sexual, evaporated. Tim's response was to put more of his energy into his job because that's where he received the most affirmation. MaryEllen knew that tenure didn't come easy and if she wanted to secure her career, she needed to put her best foot forward for the next three years. Pressures replaced the pleasures that Tim and MaryEllen had once shared. On the eve of their second wedding anniversary, Tim and MaryEllen discussed the possibility of a separation. They were both angry. They were both lonely. MaryEllen considered moving back to Pennsyl-vania to be near her friends and family. They were disappointed in each other and in marriage. The whole thing just seemed to fall apart.

In the spring of 2001, the Center for Marriage and Family at Creighton University released a report enti-tled, "Time, Sex and Money: The First Five Years of Marriage." The report focused on the problems that young people face in the early years of their marriages. The most frequently reported problem was the difficulty in balancing family and career. The second area of concern among newlyweds was the frequency of sexual relations, followed by concerns regarding money. Like so many of their peers, Tim and MaryEllen struggled to find the time to nurture their relationship while trying to meet the demands of their jobs, their families, and their finances.

A strong sexual relationship is an important bonder in marriage, but as all couples eventually discover, a healthy sexual relationship has to be integrated into the demands of daily responsibilities. Dual careers can sometimes compromise a couple's relationship. So can children, in-laws, financial concerns, and just about everything else under the sun.

A sexual relationship can nourish two people; it can provide a respite and a refuge from the pressure of everyday life. But couples need to prioritize their lives with that in mind. Sexual intimacy doesn't just happen. It's an outcome of good communication and a genuine concern for the other's wellbeing. It springs from unselfishness and a deep need to give and receive pleasure from the other. At times, great sex can require great planning. A successful marriage takes as much work as a successful career.

Jesus' Teaching

By the time Jesus walked the earth, the sexual mores of first century Israel were clearly defined. Many people seem to think that Jesus had something to do with that. Not likely. Jesus' message wasn't about sexual conduct. It was about the coming of God's kingdom. He invited people to change their hearts and their lives. Jesus asked people to live for the kingdom of God and not for their own kingdom. A commitment to this kind of life would transform every dimension of human existence, including human sexuality.

If Jesus spoke to sexual conduct, it was more in his actions than in his words. His attitudes toward women were strikingly different than most men of his day. Jesus struck up a conversation with the Samaritan woman at the well, a clear breach of society's standards. Not only did he enter into conversation with her, he revealed to her the Messianic secret.

Jesus stopped the stoning of the adulterous woman. He chose women as his friends; Mary, Martha, and Mary Magdalene. It was women who stood strong at the foot of the cross and women who discovered the empty tomb. And who does the Resurrected Christ appear to first? A woman, Mary Magdalene. Jesus challenged the social standards of his day by the way he thought and the way he acted. He didn't preach about pre-marital sex or homosexuality. He preached justice and mercy in relationships. He challenged us to maintain the dignity of every human being so that it continually reflects the image of God. Jesus said, "You have heard that it was said, 'You shall not commit adultery.' But I say to you that everyone who looks at a woman with lust has already committed adultery with her in his heart" (Matthew 5:27-28). Jesus took the law of Moses a step further than most men wanted him to go. Adultery was forbidden, but Jesus wanted us to know that demeaning a woman with disrespectful stares and sounds was also wrong. Don't commit adultery; be faithful in marriage, but also be faithful to God's creation by maintaining respect for men and women made in his image.

Sexuality and the Catholic Tradition

One of the great ironies of the Christian tradition has been its ambivalence concerning human sexuality. Christianity is rooted in the mystery of the Incarnation which says that God became fully human in the person of Jesus Christ. The sacred mystery of God took on flesh in its entirety. Yet our attitude toward the flesh has been mixed. On the one hand, the attitude is perfectly understandable. This is not the Garden of Eden and our sexual drives, urges, thoughts, and actions can be profoundly disordered. Sexuality is a powerful force, not easily controlled, that can lead us to act in ways that violate human dignity rather than enhance it. Sex can be an expression of profound intimacy and love, but it can also be an expression of violence, manipulation, or abuse. Like any of God' s gifts, sex can be misused, and because it can be misused, it didn't take long before the Christian tradition began to speak of human sexuality in negative terms. It adopted a dualistic approach to the human person which distinguished between body and soul. The soul was eternal and honorable. The body was of the earth and perishable. Sexual pleasure and sexual love belonged to the "lower" instincts of our humanity. One of the greatest theologians in history, St. Augustine, seemed to focus more on sex's power to tempt than its power to transform. For Augustine, the purpose of sex was exclusively for procreation. It was a necessary evil. Even in marriage it remained mildly sinful. This mentality has endured, on and off, to greater and lesser extents, throughout Church history. In addition, Augustine and many Fathers of the Church followed Paul's lead in teaching the superiority of celibacy to marriage. But remember, Paul thought the end of time was near, therefore, all efforts should be made to remain celibate while focusing on the coming of the Kingdom. One would get the impression that celibacy made people truly spiritual and marriage made them less holy.

At the Second Vatican Council, the Church taught officially at the highest level that sex in marriage has a dual function: it's an expression of mutual love between the partners intended to draw them closer together in intimate love as well as opening the couple to the possibility of new life. These two dimensions are often referred to as the unitive and procreative meanings of sexual intercourse. Likewise, the Council taught that the entire Church is called to a life of holiness, casting aside the notion of a spiritual caste system where married people are inferior to celibates.

A Contemporary Catholic Theology of Sexuality in Marriage

Most Catholic theologians today speak of the meaning of human sexuality in a context of marital love. Sexual intercourse belongs in marriage because it is first and foremost the ultimate form of "body language." Sex is like a sacrament within marriage. With their bodies, a married couple express their committed love. Their bed is a holy place. Sex is a profound expression of a profound commitment.

The reason that the Church links sex and marriage to each other is because they deserve each other. Sexual intimacy and emotional intimacy go hand-in-hand in marriage. Of course, as every married person knows, we don't live on the mountaintop. The intimacy, love, and joy of sex will go through peaks and valleys just as the relationship will go through peaks and valleys. The sexual relationship will often serve as a barometer of the personal relationship which will ebb and flow throughout the life of the marriage. It's unrealistic to enter into marriage without the recognition that human sexuality develops and changes over time, as does sexual expression. At its best, however, sex can remain a deep form of human love and intimate bonding.

The procreative meaning of sexual intercourse is no longer understood as its sole purpose, but it remains intrinsically connected to both sexual intercourse and marriage. A common misconception of a time gone by was to believe that every act of intercourse in marriage must intend procreation. The Church teaches that couples have the right and responsibility to limit the size of their families according to their emotional and financial limitations. The relationship is ideally procreative. It's open to bringing new life into the world. The Catholic Church has always taught that the miracle of a child is best suited to the miracle of wedded love between a man and woman. There are, of course, many other ways in which marriage can be lifegiving, but the gift of a child remains a living sign of married love.

Chapter Eight

Planning a Family

IF there's one area of marriage preparation that leaves presenting couples a little uneasy, it's the issue of birth control. It's a difficult topic for a number of reasons, beginning with the fact that engaged couples aren't coming to marriage preparation classes with questions about family planning. Sociological data tells us that most young couples today are sexually active long before marriage. If that's true, then the question of birth control is raised somewhere during courtship and settled long before engagement. Young couples come to marriage preparation with very little interest in discussing birth control and with even less interest in hearing what a celibate male hierarchy has to say about it. That's unfortunate because a discussion on birth control can be nestled in a broader discussion on conscience, decision making, and the couple's health and communication patterns in a way that can truly benefit the couple.

Our experience tells us that the engaged couples aren't the only ones who are resistant to raising the issue of birth control. We've found that married couples are sometimes uncomfortable with the Church's teaching on birth control or are unfamiliar with *Humanae Vitae*, the encyclical on the regulation of birth authored by Pope Paul VI in 1968. They may also be unfamiliar with the specifics of Natural Family Planning or they may falsely believe that the Church insists upon married couples having unlimited numbers of children. It's important to remember, however, that ministry is more than sharing our personal stories. Ministry requires sharing the Church's story, as well. Therefore, participation in the ministry of marriage preparation obligates us to know the teaching of the Church and to communicate it to engaged couples. Many parish programs fulfill this obligation by contacting the diocesan office that sponsors Natural Family Planning and requesting that a teaching couple visit their parish.

Before we were married, we attended a seminar on NFP sponsored by our diocese. The method was beautifully presented by married couples who had used NFP throughout their marriages and were then certified as NFP instructors. We received charts and a thermometer and a detailed explanation of how to use them to help us better understand the reproductive cycle. We also received a profound respect for procreation.

The human body is remarkable. Learning how it works, particularly how it signals fertility and infertility, reminded us that God's creation is nothing less than perfect. Learning how to use Natural Family Planning changed the way we understood our relationship, our sexuality, and even the way we've raised our children. Our daughters, both teenagers now, understand themselves and the physical and psychological changes that they've experienced in recent years better than most girls their age. We've been able to explain those changes in a way that most parents can't because most couples are not aware of the cyclical changes that take place in a woman's body. Our daughters know when and why they're ovulating and they can anticipate the physical and emotional changes that accompany this phase of their cycles each month. Hopefully, they too, have gained a more profound respect for the nature of sexuality as a result of understanding exactly how their reproductive cycles work.

Many people do not know that NFP is the umbrella term that includes the sympto-thermal method (STM), ovulation method (OM), and the basal body temperature (BBT). Each method is scientifically based. Natural Family Planning is not rhythm, a primitive family planning method that was more attentive to the calendar than it was to a woman's natural signs of fertility and infertility. Rhythm was not effective either, whereas both the World Health Organization and the U.S. Department of Health and Human Services were able to confirm that NFP boasts a method effectiveness rate of 97-98 percent, and estimated user effectiveness at 85-95 percent. Compare these figures to the reliability of artificial forms of birth control. You might be surprised to learn that NFP is as effective as most forms of artificial contraception, and even more effective than some commonly used forms of birth control.

NFP is safe and takes into consideration both the physical and psychological wellbeing of a woman's body. It can be used confidently by all women, even women who are at risk for strokes or cancer. The birth control pill has been linked with medical side effects ranging from blood clots to breast cancer. The I.U.D. can cause cramping, bleeding, or pelvic inflammation. Spermicidal foams and condoms can cause vaginal irritation and be uncomfortable. Health conscious young adults might be interested in a form of family planning that promotes their wellbeing. We've read many articles in secular publications, particularly women's magazines, featuring NFP as a method of family planning that is gaining popularity among younger couples, both couples who are trying to avoid a pregnancy and couples who are struggling to achieve a pregnancy. Because a woman gains a heightened awareness of her body through NFP, she is capable of detecting changes in her body that might help her identify the presence of a wide range of medical problems sooner than most women. Many women are encouraged by their gynecologists to register for a course in NFP when they are experiencing difficulty conceiving. Before seeking out more serious procedures at an infertility clinic, couples are often pointed in the direction of the Catholic Church where they can be taught to identify signs of fertility or infertility.

Because I was in tune with my body's changes, I knew that I was pregnant within days of conception. Ovulation raises a woman's body temperature. If conception takes place, her body temperature remains elevated. Because I had this information, I was able to begin taking pre-natal vitamins and making a conscious effort to avoid alcohol and other environmental stressors that can pose a threat to a developing fetus immediately following conception. We believe that our children received the benefits of NFP right from the start.

NFP is not aggressively advertised the way artificial contraceptives are, therefore, the general population is not aware that NFP exists. We've found that oftentimes NFP is not even mentioned in high school or college level sex education programs, which is unfortunate because both males and females would benefit from being better informed about the reproductive cycle. They might develop a deeper appreciation for the genius of God's creation, and who knows, that sense of awe might impact other problems that are so common among young people today, including sexually transmitted diseases, HIV, and unplanned pregnancies.

For more information on NFP, contact your diocese, or any one of the following resources listed below.

Secretariat for Pro-Life Activities, National Conference of Catholic Bishops/United States Catholic Conference

3211 Fourth Street, N.E.,
Washington, DC 20017-1194
Phone (202) 541-3070
or online: http://www.nccbuscc.org

Diocesan Development Program for Natural Family
Planning
3211 Fourth Street, N.E.
Washington, DC 20017-1194
Phone: (202) 541-3240/3070
Fax: (202) 541-3054

Pope Paul VI Institute
6901 Mercy Road
Omaha, NE 68106-2604
Phone: (402) 390-6600
Fax: (402) 390-9851

Newsletter, brochures, books, conference information,
presentations slides, videos, and audiotapes available.

Natural Family Planning Center of Washington, D.C.
8514 Bradmoor Dr., Bethesda, MD 20817-3810
Phone: (301) 897-9323
Fax: (301) 571-5267
e-mail: hklaus@dgsys.com

Couple to Couple League (CCL)—International /USA
PO Box 111184
Cincinnati, OH 45211
Phone (513) 471-2000
Fax: (513) 557-2449
Online http://www.ccli.org

Chapter Nine

Talk to Me

RESEARCH indicates that the single best predictor of a happy marriage is the quality of the communication between spouses. In fact, John Gottman, a professor of psychology at the University of Washington and author of several books on marital communication, claims that divorce can be predicted with 90 percent accuracy by scrutinizing the pre-marital patterns of communication between the bride and groom-to-be. Gottman has spent thirty years studying couple's communication patterns. With the use of videotapes and body sensors, he has carefully monitored, not just the words couples choose when trying to communicate, but their body language and emotional responses, as well. Too often, the engaged couple comes into the relationship repeating poor patterns of communication and conflict resolution that were learned in their families of origin. They will most likely model their parents' communication patterns until the marriage prep team models something different. This can be done in a variety of ways. One way is for two members of the marriage prep team to role play an argument using communication strategies that have been proven to be effective. Another way is to video tape the engaged couple trying to work through a difficulty in their relationship and review it after the group has presented alternative communication styles that can be used in resolving conflict. If taping the engaged couples is too burdensome, then perhaps the team can obtain video-tapes of other couples resolving conflicts. Couples tend to make a lot of similar mistakes when arguing. The engaged couples might be able to identify some of the mistakes that they make while viewing other couples saying and doing the things they do in the heat of an animated discussion.

Howard Markman and Scott Stanley, Directors of the Center for Marital and Family Studies at the University of Denver, spent twenty years studying couple communication and its impact on the success or failure of a relationship. Their years of research emerged as PREP, The Prevention and Relationship Enhancement Program, which teaches couples how to communicate effectively and manage conflicts without damaging their relationship. Markman and Stanley, along with Susan Blumberg, authored *Fighting For Your Marriage,* a book, videotape, and audiotape designed to teach couples the strategies and techniques of communication patterns outlined in PREP.

One of the clever strategies presented is a 5 x 5 plastic floor tile called The Floor. Each couple receives a tile with the Speaker-Listener Technique written on it. The Speaker-Listener Technique is a simple set of rules designed to guide a couple's conversation, particularly when an argument ensues. For example, one of the rules written on The Floor is use "I" statements that communicate only your own thoughts and feelings. Another rule is let the Listener take time to re-state what the Speaker has just said without offering any opinions or judgments. Both parties will have their turn to speak when The Floor is passed from Speaker to Listener.

The Floor is a simple tool that prevents both people from speaking at the same time. Let's face it, when an argument breaks out, both parties want to be heard and no one really wants to listen. So what happens? Both husband and wife begin to shout to be heard over the other. PREP reminds the couple that only one person can talk at a time. The Floor is a prop to help reinforce that behavior. Sounds simple enough, and yet, so many couples forget the simple rules of communication when they get angry. The PREP authors are convinced that it's not what couples argue about that destroys their relationship, it's how they argue that rips the relationship apart. To order *Fighting For Your Marriage,* call 1-800-366-0166.

When Dolores Curran conducted research for her 1983 book, *Traits of a Healthy Family,* she asked professionals working with families; psychologists, pediatricians, family physicians, social workers, principals, teachers, clergy, coaches, and volunteers from a variety of backgrounds, to identify the traits of a healthy family. The trait that was identified by her respondents as most important was communication. Curran's findings were consistent with the data published by the National Study of Family Strengths. What is it about the way a healthy family communicates that sets it apart from an unhealthy family? Feelings are communicated freely and positively, allowing each member of the family to take risks and maintain strong self esteem. Eventually the children in these families will take the risks necessary to become independent and form healthy relationships outside the home.

Curran also discovered that her respondents felt that the healthy family had control over interruptions in their communication, such as the TV and telephone. Couples and other family members will always have to talk louder if they are competing with the television or stereo. The healthy family will be able to identify the things in their environment that distract them from clear, comfortable communication with each other. They will be able to prioritize their need to communicate with each other and differentiate that from being in a room together, focusing on the thoughts and feelings of TV personalities rather than those of the people in the room with them. The healthy family is also able to recognize non-verbal communication and respond appropriately. Is the husband aware that his wife wants to talk about her day if he comes home and turns on the news right away? Is his wife able to acknowledge that her husband would like to talk about his day if she's on the phone or online talking to everyone else when her husband comes home? Each couple will develop their own way of signaling that they need time alone with their spouse, but the couple also needs to develop ways in which they can recognize both the non-verbal and verbal cues that the other is sending.

Thomas Peters and Robert Waterman, Jr., authors of *In Search of Excellence,* claim that easy communication was one of the hallmarks of companies that excel. "The nature and uses of communication in excellent companies are remarkably different from those of their non-excellent peers. The excellent companies are a vast network of informal, open communications." Healthy corporations foster independent thinking and free communication. So do healthy families. There is an ease of interaction within both the healthy family and the thriving corporation. It would seem that both outstanding businesses and outstanding families have good, clear, open communication, both verbal and non-verbal, at their core.

Stephen Covey, author of *The 7 Habits of Highly Effective People* agrees. "Communication is the most important skill in life." Following the huge success of his first book, Covey published *The 7 Habits of Highly Effective Families,* recommended reading for professionals working with couples and families today. His book also makes a wonderful gift for a young couple just starting to build their family.

Those of us involved in marriage preparation today are fortunate to have access to the information emerging from empirical research on couples' communication. We would be wise to incorporate the findings of Gottman, of Markman and Stanley, Curran, Covey, and sociologists such as Deborah Tannen, whose 1990 book, *You Just Don't Understand: Women and Men in Conversation,* drew our attention to the gender differences in communication patterns. Tannen is a professor of linguistics at Georgetown University who has done groundbreaking work in the area of conversational styles of men and women. Not unlike John Gray, whose body of work, beginning with *Men are From Mars, Women are From Venus,* swept the world by storm with his engaging presentation of gender differences in communication styles. He has several videotapes on the market, even in your public library, which could serve as an introduction to a session on couples' communication. We've found that young couples are familiar with Gray's work and his popular style of presentation. His videos are entertaining and put everyone at ease.

Remember, if our deepest relational needs cannot be met in marriage, we look elsewhere. Engaged couples can benefit tremendously from learning the skills necessary for optimum communication and conflict resolution.

Chapter Ten

Interfaith Marriage

TEVYE, the poor milkman whose music and musings brought the story of the Jewish people to Broadway, disowned his daughter for marrying a gentile. *Fiddler on the Roof* brought us back to a time when hearts could be broken, but tradition could not.

When a Jewish Woody Allen wooed a WASP named Annie Hall, the striking differences between the ill-fated, interfaith couple left us all laughing. When romance and religious differences surface on stage and screen, emotions range from hilarity to heartache. But what about in real life?

It seems to be more heartache. It's difficult to pinpoint the reasons for an 80 percent divorce rate among interfaith couples, but the couples themselves and the experts who have worked closely with them have offered some speculation.

Religious beliefs can shape our views on life, death, love, sex, money, and children as well as determine who we are, what we eat, how we speak, where we live and how we see ourselves. The differences between an Irish Catholic bride and a Jewish groom whose ancestors came from Russia may extend far beyond their religious affiliation. Ethnicity and religious background play a significant role in the formation of family dynamics. For example, families whose cultural heritage is northern European may value independence more than a Jewish family from the Middle East where the boundaries are more fluid and members are more enmeshed. Initially, an Irish or English groom may be attracted to the closeness of his bride's Jewish family, but in time, he might find the extended family involvement to be smothering. What the Jewish wife sees as reserve and respect for personal space may later be perceived as distance and a lack of concern for her or her children. Many times people fall in love with a quality they see in a partner that is lacking in themselves. Later on, it can be a source of division.

The young girl who has had difficulty separating from her overbearing parents may use an interfaith marriage as a symbol of independence and liberation from mom and dad. Marrying out of one's faith could be the result of simply falling in love with a particular person, or it could be a rejection of one's family or a particular way of life.

An interfaith couple may have fewer shared memories of childhood and family gatherings. Their educational experiences were probably different, as were their holidays, the food they ate, the manner in which they celebrated or mourned. A Jewish girl may have grieved the passing of her grandmother by sitting shiva and sharing fond memories aloud while her Catholic boyfriend mourned his grandfather's death at a wake where family and friends told funny stories of the deceased. Perhaps death and the powerful emotions it evokes were shared openly in one family and silenced in the other. When a Jewish bride and a Catholic groom marry, they may have much more to learn about each other than they think.

Rifts in an interfaith marital relationship may surface over the difference between a menorah and a manger, but chances are, there's more at stake than a religious symbol. Holidays hold potent memories, and at some point the interfaith couple might realize that their differences are not just religious, but emotional, philosophical, social and psychological, as well. Marriage counselors, psychiatrists, clergy and interfaith couples themselves agree that religion is hardly ever the cause of severe, protracted marital conflicts, but rather a smokescreen for power struggles and unfinished business from their families of origin. Religious differences are often an easy scapegoat for many marital ills that have their roots elsewhere. For this reason, special attention must be given to the interfaith couple preparing for marriage.

Some parishes and dioceses have initiated interfaith marriage preparation programs. The Church recognizes that all couples need to work at integrating issues of personality, family histories, and communication, but interfaith couples face the unique challenge of having to explore some issues sooner than other couples.

In *Faithful to Each Other Forever,* the Catholic bishops addressed the specific needs of interfaith couples, but in doing so, they first tried to clarify the awkward ambiguity surrounding the terms used to describe marriages between Catholics and those who are non-Catholics. Many people use the terms ecumenical, interdenominational, mixed, interchurch, or interfaith interchangeably. The bishops use the word interreligious as a generic term to cover any marriage that involves a Roman Catholic and a partner who is not Roman Catholic. Interreligious includes the marriage of a Catholic and a Christian from another denomination, such as Lutheran or Methodist, as well as from another faith, such as Judaism or Hinduism. Two people who share the Christian faith, Protestants and Catholics alike, are not entering into an interfaith marriage. Theirs is sometimes referred to as an interdenominational or interchurch marriage. If both parties have been baptized as Christians, regardless of the denomination, they still share the Christian faith. They share many of the same religious holidays and their liturgies are similar. The marriage between a Roman Catholic and a non-baptized person, such as a Jew or a Muslim, would be considered an interfaith marriage. They do not share the gospels or the same holidays and their worship would have a different focus.

The Church asks that the Catholic spouse promise to do all in his or her power to have the children of any interreligious marriage raised as Catholics. This promise takes the form of a dispensation that is signed by the Catholic before the wedding. The non-Catholic spouse need not sign the dispensation, but he or she must be aware that the Catholic has made such a promise. It is the Church's belief that a Catholic person's relationship to Christ is so important that it should be shared with his or her children.

The conversation regarding children is an important one to raise in an interfaith marriage preparation program. A child cannot be raised as both a Christian and a non-Christian. The fundamentals of faith are different. When Joan Rivers' daughter, Melissa, got engaged to a Christian, she asked the God Squad, the popular interfaith celebrities, Rabbi Marc Gelman and Monsignor Tom Hartman, to witness their wedding. When Rabbi Gelman interviewed Melissa regarding the religious formation of her children, she said that she would raise her children as both Christian and Jewish. The rabbi, who conducted this interview on TV, challenged the bride-to-be. How can you raise a child to believe in Jesus as the messiah and at the same time pray for the coming of the messiah? The God Squad declined the invitation to participate in the wedding on the premise that a child cannot be both Christian and Jewish. Children can join in the celebrations of their grandparents and learn to appreciate and respect the faiths of both sides of the family, but it is important that the child form his or her own religious identity. Hopefully, the interfaith couple can decide this before the wedding so that the pregnancy and birth of their firstborn is not compromised by arguments that extend to relatives on both sides.

The announcement that an interfaith couple are expecting a child can elicit emotions that range from complete joy to utter craziness. Relatives run the gamut from tirades to tears, from currish disagreement to complete disengagement. There can be shouting or silence, war or withdrawal. Both fighting and distancing are common attempts to manage anxiety in a situation like this, although neither are very effective. When children fall in love with someone of another faith parents can feel sad, guilty, disappointed, or threatened. Jewish parents and grandparents might perceive an interfaith marriage as a threat to the survival of Judiasm, an anguish not shared by Christian families. What is shared, however, is the fact that all parents, Jewish or Christian, Buddist or atheist, can feel that their children's choices are a reflection of their success or failure as a parent. Jewish parents can feel the guilt of having betrayed their ancestors when there is no bris for their grandchild; Christian grandparents can feel frightened for the salvation of their grandchild if there is no baptism. There may be disappointment all around because grandchildren will not share the customs and traditions that have been part of a family's fabric for generations.

The couple must be able to acknowledge that a wedding represents the joining of two families, the heritage and histories, the customs and celebrations. Showing sensitivity to the reactions of parents or grandparents, siblings or cousins, could enhance family communication before and long after the wedding. But in the end, the couple must choose according to their consciences, consciences that have been informed by the wisdom of the Church and the experiences of interfaith couples and those who have worked closely with them.

Interfaith marriage preparation sessions provide the engaged couple with the opportunity to discuss the joys and challenges of interfaith family life with interfaith couples who have been where these young couples are going. The engaged couples who attend an interfaith program will also meet other young couples who are facing the same set of circumstances as themselves. They can exchange ideas for the ceremony and helpful hints in dealing with in-laws. And most of all, they can find camaraderie in celebrating the blessings of an interfaith marriage; the acceptance of differences and the opportunities to grow in ways they wouldn't if they married within their faith. Both faiths can be vitalized by the conscientious way in which both the bride and groom examine their religious background and its importance in their life.

The most recent statistics tell us that the number of Catholic weddings in the United States are decreasing every year. One reason seems to be that more and more Catholics are marrying non-Catholics and those weddings have traditionally been more likely to take place outside of the Church. Years ago, a non-Catholic often converted to Catholicism before the marriage. Today, the trend has reversed itself or evened out. Catholics are converting to the faith of their non-Catholic spouse at least as often as non-Catholics are seeking to become Catholics. Of course, only those interreligious couples who have chosen a Catholic wedding will attend our Pre-Cana programs. Throughout the United States, an average of 30 percent of the couples registering for these programs will be interreligious couples. Demographics will decide the numbers. When Catholics comprise a large number of the general population of an area, the number of interreligious weddings are fewer than in an area where Catholics make up a small percent of the general population. For example, in the diocese of Brownsville, Texas, where Catholics make up 81 percent of the population, the intermarriage rate is lower than the national average rate of 30 percent. However, in areas such as Lafayette, Indiana, where Catholics only make up 8 percent of the general population, the intermarriage rate is over 50 percent.

We're not the only ones with our eyes on the numbers. In some parts of the United States, almost 80 percent of Jews are marrying non-Jews, an alarming statistic for the Jewish community. Not only are the rabbis and religious Jews raising their concerns around interfaith marriages, but secular Jews such as Alan Dershowitz, the outspoken Harvard law professor, are entering the discussion, as well. His book, *The Vanishing American Jew,* claims that intermarriage, low birth rates, and assimilation will bring about the end of American Judaism. Dershowitz was raised as an Orthodox Jew, raised his children as secular Jews, and now has a son who is married to a Catholic. Studies indicate that fewer than 20 percent of Jews who marry outside Judaism raise their children as Jews. A generation later, fewer than five percent of those children raise their children Jewish. The fear among Jews is that their faith will be lost in America.

But these issues are of little concern to many of the young interfaith couples who are choosing to marry. They're in love and they believe that love knows no bounds. Let's provide them with resources that will support them in their journey. *Dovetail* is a wonderful journal by and for Jewish/Christian families. A subscription makes an ideal wedding gift for the interfaith couple. For information regarding Interfaith Support Groups around the United States, audio and video tapes, Dovetail's National Conference, books and other resources, contact The Dovetail Institute for Interfaith Family Resources, 775 Simon Greenwell Lane, Boston, KY 40107, 1-800-530-1596, dovetailinstitute.org.

Chapter Eleven

The Wedding Liturgy

Msgr. Ronald Hayde

PREPARING couples to plan and then to celebrate their wedding liturgy can be a daunting task. The liturgy provides so many options. Parish to parish can differ in their local policies. Some couples have a familiarity with the mechanics of liturgy planning, others have virtually no familiarity at all. This chapter attempts to look at some of the issues that couples will face in planning their wedding liturgy, together with some guidance that will hopefully make the planning experience profitable and the celebration of the wedding liturgy a joyful event.

My Wedding vs. the Church's Wedding

The wedding liturgy is at one and the same time both a personal event and an ecclesial event. As a personal event, it involves the couple who will be intimately joined in marriage, along with their families and friends who have journeyed with them. As an ecclesial event, the wedding liturgy is a rite of the church, and, as such, draws the individual couple into the wider circle of the church celebrating the presence of God in this particular marriage covenant. While this may seen terribly obvious, this starting point is often the cause of many a battle and hurt feelings when one aspect overshadows the other. In most other aspects of preparing for their marriage, the couple has been told that they can have whatever they want. While it may come with a price, the couple is normally told that "this is their day" and they should feel free to do whatever they need to do. When arriving to plan the wedding liturgy, the church provides certain parameters that can initially be viewed as obstacles. With a basic understanding of the personal and ecclesial dimensions of the marriage liturgy, couples approaching liturgy preparation can avoid many pitfalls. Both the personal and ecclesial are held in tension.

The Eucharist (Nuptial Mass) or Wedding Ceremony (Service of the Word)

While the most fitting context for the celebration of the marriage of two Catholics is the Eucharist, this is not always possible or advisable. The dwindling number of priests, and the large number of already scheduled Masses may preclude the option of celebrating the marriage within the context of the Eucharist. If the couple does not participate in the Eucharistic life of the church at this time, it would seem advisable for them to celebrate their marriage in the context of a Service of the Word.

Scripture Readings

The Lectionary for the Rite of Marriage provides a variety of scripture readings for use at weddings. There are several popular preparation aids that provide the texts of these readings. The wealth of options can leave many a couple flustered. They should be advised to spend some time looking over the readings. The parish priest, deacon, or parish liturgy coordinator can often help them narrow down the options. It would be important for the couple to know that it is not permitted to replace any of the scriptural readings with non-Scriptural readings.

Other Liturgical Texts

The variable texts of the liturgy (Prayers, Intercessions, Preface, Nuptial Blessing, Final Blessing) can also be selected by the couple. For those familiar with the church's liturgy, many couples would find one text speaks more clearly to them and their marriage than another. For others less familiar, the task of selecting the texts can appear overwhelming. In such cases, it might be best to let the priest or deacon select the texts.

The Exchange of Vows

The Rite of Marriage provides two forms for the exchange of vows: the first, or active form, in which the couple pronounce the vows directly to each other (or repeat them after the officiant) in the midst of the church community. The second, or passive form, has the couple respond to the questions posed by the officiant.

What does the ritual formula look like? The "active form" states: I, n., take you, n., to be my wife. I promise to be true to you in good times and in bad, in sickness and in health. I will love you and honor you all the days of my life. The "passive form" would take the active form text and put it into the form of a question, to which the bride and groom respond, "I do."

Using the words of the church, the exchange of vows is a public act, binding the couple to the faith of the whole church. The ritual formula should not be set aside for an individual formula written by the couple. The ritual form preserves the integrity of both the church's liturgy and the church's belief about marriage. I can recall one wedding where as a member of the assembly, I listened to the couple promise to remain faithful to each other as long as the sun shone. It certainly raised some interesting questions.

Music

There is probably no aspect of the wedding liturgy that presents more challenges than music. Most parishes have some sort of policy concerning the music done at weddings. Many of these policies contain a good deal of flexibility. Couples would be well advised to read the parish policy and enter into conversation with the parish musician(s) well in advance of their wedding date.

Music in the liturgy should be good music, music that supports the nature of the liturgy and the liturgical action, and music that will enable the assembled people to express their faith.

The texts of the music ought to express not only the human dimensions of love, but the divine as well. While many popular songs might be a favorite of a particular couple, such songs might be more appropriately used at the wedding reception.

Ministers

Readers

The proclamation of God's word is a significant part of the wedding liturgy. Family members or friends can be chosen to serve as readers, but this choice ought not to be made in haste. Couples should be encouraged to look to people who might already serve as readers, or to those who have some experience with public speaking. To some this might be a statement of the obvious, but many a wedding has had a "reader" struggle with great effort to get through a reading that the person never should have been asked to do in the first place.

The couple should be reminded to provide a copy of the reading to the reader in advance.

Special Ministers of the Eucharist

If the wedding liturgy is celebrated in the context of the Eucharist, and if there is a family member or friend who has been commissioned as a Special Minister of the Eucharist, the couple should let the priest know this, and address whatever parish or diocesan policy might be in effect.

Ushers

Traditionally groomsmen function as ushers. They can, in fact, be the ministers of hospitality to the guests who arrive for the wedding. It would be helpful if the couple could inform the ushers about special seating arrangements, the location of restrooms, and any other details that might arise.

Other Customs

There are many popular customs and cultural customs that have found their way into the wedding liturgy. Some of these customs are the use of a wedding or unity candle; the giving of roses to mothers/parents; the placing of flowers before the statue of the Virgin Mary; crowning the bride and groom. These customs, while secondary in the marriage liturgy, are not prohibited. Couples ought to use one of these because of the particular meaning it holds for them, not just for the sake of adding onto the celebration.

Photographers/Videographers

Most couples spend a significant amount of money on photographers and videographers. Many parishes have a policy concerning how photographers and videographers may function in the church building. To avoid disappointment, couples should be advised to seek out the parish policy, if there is one, and communicate that policy to the people they have hired for these services.

Occasionally a couple will receive an offer from a family member to photograph or video the wedding liturgy. It would be important for this individual to be aware of any parish policies that might exist. In addition it would be important for that person to cooperate with the hired photographer/videographer. I can recall looking at the pictures of one couple's wedding to find their much beloved uncle, who was an amateur photographer, in virtually every picture, shown attempting to take a picture. When he was not in the picture, some part of his body or his extensive camera equipment always managed to be there.

Preparing a Booklet

The booklet for the wedding liturgy serves as both a participation aid and a memento of the occasion. The booklet is not a word-for-word script of the wedding liturgy. It is helpful for couples to see copies of previous wedding booklets as they begin to prepare their own. Making these sample booklets available can save many a couple several weeks of anxiety.

Interreligious/Interchurch Ceremonies

Interreligious/Interchurch Ceremonies involve a Catholic and a non-Catholic Christian. When the priest or deacon is present along with the other Christian minister, the general rule of thumb would be that the marriage ritual of the officiant is followed. In other words, the home ground of the officiant usually provides the ritual. The other clergyperson be it priest, deacon, or other Christian minister can offer prayers and blessings.

Interfaith Ceremonies

Interfaith ceremonies involve a Catholic and a non-Christian. When the priest or deacon is present along with a non-Christian minister, the general rule of thumb would be that the marriage ritual of the officiant is followed. This does not preclude the other minister from participating in the scripture readings, or from offering prayers and blessings. Couples who will be married in interfaith ceremonies are well advised to discuss the issues surrounding the ceremony with the officiant well in advance of the ceremony. Most often the two clergypersons involved will work out the details.

When the Catholic is the officiant of an interfaith marriage, the liturgy takes place in the context of a Service of the Word, not the Eucharist. A dispensation can be granted for this wedding to take place outside a church building, in such places as an interfaith chapel or catering hall. This is often done to avoid offending the sensibilities of family members.

No list is exhaustive. There are certainly other areas where we could give some direction to couples who are approaching the preparation of their wedding liturgy. I do think, however, that these are some of the prime areas that will demand their attention. If we can encourage couples to approach the liturgy preparations with a spirit of patience, openness, charity, and above all, a sense of humor, I think we will have done a fine job of setting the stage for the work of liturgy preparation.

BIBLIOGRAPHY

Center for Marriage and Family at Creighton University, *Time, Sex and Money: The First Five Years of Marriage,* 2001.

Covey, Stephen *The 7 Habits of Highly Effective Families,* Golden Books, 1997.

_____. *The 7 Habits of Highly Effective People,* Simon and Schuster, 1989.

Curran, Dolores. *Traits of a Healthy Family,* Winston Press, 1983.

Gottman, John. *The Relationship Cure: A Five Step Guide to Building Better Connections With Family, Friends and Lovers,* Crown Publishing Group, 2001.

_____. *What Predicts Divorce? The Relationship Between Marital Processes and Marital Outcomes,* Lawrence Erlbaum Assoc., 1993

_____. *Why Marriages Succeed or Fail and How You Can Make Yours Last,* Simon & Schuster,1994.

Gray, John. *Mars and Venus in Love: Inspiring and Heartfelt Stories of Relationships,* Harper Collins Publishers, 1996.

_____. *Men are From Mars, Women are From Venus,* Harper Collins, 1992.

Groome, Thomas H. *Sharing Faith,* Harper Collins, 1991.

John Paul II. *Familiaris Consortio,* (On the Family), December 15, 1981.

Markman, Stanley, and Blumberg. *Fighting for Your Marriage,* Jossey Bass, Inc., 1994. To order call 1-800-366-0166.

NCCB/USCC. *Faithful to Each Other Forever, A Catholic Handbook of Pastoral Help for Marriage Preparation,* No. 252-7.

_____. *Growing Together in Spirit,* No. 353-1, 48 pages, $2.95

_____. *Making Marriage Work,* No. 355-8, 48 pages, $2.95

_____. *Natural Family Planning,* National Standards of the National Conference of Catholic Bishops Diocesan Development Program, No. 395-7, 32 pages, $3.95

_____. *Our Future Together,* No. 351-5, 72 pages, $3.95

_____. *Planning Your Wedding Ceremony,* No. 354-X, 48 pages, $2.95

_____. *Sons and Daughters of the Light: A Pastoral Plan for Ministry with Young Adults,* 1996.

Paul VI. *Humanae Vitae,* (On the Regulation of Birth) Encyclical Letter, July 25, 1968.

Peters, Thomas J. and Robert H. Waterman, Jr. *In Search of Excellence,* Warner Books, 1982.

Tannen, Deborah. *Gender and Conversational Interaction,* Oxford University Press, 1993.

_____. *You Just Don't Understand: Women and Men in Conversation,* Ballantine Books, 1990.

Wallerstein, Judith, Julia Lewis, and Sandra Blakeslee. *The Unexpected Legacy of Divorce: A 25 Year Landmark Study,* Hyperion, 2000.

RESOURCES

For more information on FOCCUS, contact The Family Life Office:

Archdiocese of Omaha
3214 N. 60th Street
Omaha, NE 68104
(402) 551-9003

For more information on the pastoral formation of marriage preparation teams contact:

Lauren Hanley, S.J.
Office of Pastoral Formation
50 North Park Avenue
Rockville Centre, NY 11590
(516) 678-5800

Dovetail, A Journal by and for Jewish/Christian Families:

Dovetail Institute
775 Simon Greenwell Lane
Boston, KY 40107
(800) 530-1596
dovetailinstitute.org

PREP or Christian PREP
P.O. Box 102530
Denver, CO 80250-2530
(303) 759-9931
e-mail: PREPinfo@aol.com

Additional Titles Published by Resurrection Press, a Catholic Book Publishing Imprint

A Rachel Rosary *Larry Kupferman*	$4.50
Blessings All Around *Dolores Leckey*	$8.95
Catholic Is Wonderful *Mitch Finley*	$4.95
Come, Celebrate Jesus! *Francis X. Gaeta*	$4.95
Days of Intense Emotion *Keeler/Moses*	$12.95
From Holy Hour to Happy Hour *Francis X. Gaeta*	$7.95
Healing through the Mass *Robert DeGrandis, SSJ*	$9.95
The Healing Rosary *Mike D.*	$5.95
Healing Your Grief *Ruthann Williams, OP*	$7.95
Healthy and Holy Under Stress *Muto, VanKaam*	$3.95
Heart Peace *Adolfo Quezada*	$9.95
Life, Love and Laughter *Jim Vlaun*	$7.95
Living Each Day by the Power of Faith *Barbara Ryan*	$8.95
The Joy of Being a Catechist *Gloria Durka*	$4.95
The Joy of Being a Eucharistic Minister *Mitch Finley*	$5.95
The Joy of Music Ministry *John Michael Talbot*	$6.95
The Joy of Preaching *Rod Damico*	$6.95
The Joy of Ushers *Gretchen Hailer*	$5.95
Lights in the Darkness *Ave Clark, O.P.*	$8.95
Loving Yourself for God's Sake *Adolfo Quezada*	$5.95
Mother Teresa *Eugene Palumbo*	$5.95
Our Grounds for Hope *Fulton J. Sheen*	$7.95
Personally Speaking *Jim Lisante*	$8.95
Practicing the Prayer of Presence *van Kaam/Muto*	$8.95
5-Minute Miracles *Linda Schubert*	$4.95
Season of New Beginnings *Mitch Finley*	$4.95
Season of Promises *Mitch Finley*	$4.95
Stay with Us *John Mullin, SJ*	$3.95
Surprising Mary *Mitch Finley*	$7.95
What He Did for Love *Francis X. Gaeta*	$5.95
You Are My Beloved *Mitch Finley*	$10.95
Your Sacred Story *Robert Lauder*	$6.95

For a free catalog call 1-800-892-6657